To Be You Again

A Pathway to Healing from Violence

Patricia Drury Sidman, CPCC

Cover photo: "Grace" © 2013 Eric Svendson, www.ericsvendson.com

For information or permissions, contact patriciadsidman@gmail.com
Published in Lafayette, LA

ISBN-13: 978-1-5053-5417-1
ISBN-10: 150535417X

Library of Congress 2014921713
SEL001000 SELF-HELP / Abuse
1. Violence recovery 2. Guide for survivors 3. How to help survivors 4. Victim self-help 5. Trauma and recovery

A portion of the profits from the sale of this book will be donated to organizations that serve survivors of rape and domestic violence.

What Others Have Said About

To Be You Again

"Read this book. There is no other quite like it. Patricia Drury Sidman has given us a gift in this deceptively small book. It is free of judgment, full of wisdom, grounded in experience, and eminently readable: no jargon, no platitudes, no psychobabble. From her own horrific experience, Sidman knows there is courage to be found in vulnerability, and that even a broken heart, like a rose that always opens itself to the sun even when planted in a patch of weeds, can heal and bloom with careful tending. Read this book. It will change you."

~ Lyn Cowan, PhD, Jungian Analyst

"Surviving physical violence is the first step in healing from its devastating damage. Drawing from her own firsthand experience as a survivor of violence, the author [Patricia Sidman] equips the [her] reader with the tools to turn the table on powerlessness and embark on the quest to healing and wholeness. Through weaving her own powerful story with common sense, practical instructions, she gives practical guidance through every step in the recovery of body, mind and spirit to become herself again."

~ Bishop Rosamonde Ikshvàku Miller,
Ecclesia Gnostica Mysteriorum

"Patricia Sidman opened her soul for all to see. The lessons life teaches us sometimes are through seemingly unbearable experiences. And lessons she did learn and learn well. Thank you, Patricia, for not giving up, for carrying on despite the odds, and for being so generous as to publicly give this part of your soul so that others might have a chance to recover from the violence in their lives."

~ Dr. Marie Pace, Naturopathic Doctor and Author,
DISCOVER HEALTH

"Patricia Drury Sidman has written a brief, cogent book informed by a well-lived life. Her careful instructions for taking care of every piece of ourselves—and then for finding peace through letting go—will resonate far beyond the final page."

~ Sally Donlon, Assistant Dean,
College of Liberal Arts,
University of Louisiana at Lafayette

"Much of my life has been spent feeling terrified. *To Be You Again* is one of the most empowering books I have ever read. It changed my life."

~ Survivor of over 20 years of domestic abuse

*For all who suffer because their power and well-being
have been violently stolen from them*

Contents

Preface

This book is a map of one pathway through the territory of healing from violence. It contains an account of what happened to me and the similar stories of others I have known or coached over the years. If you have been the victim of violence, I wrote the book so you will know you are not alone, and you have the power to make your own life better and find new meaning and joy again. I wrote it because I know for sure that deep healing is possible. I will tell you how I know so you can believe it.

I know about surviving and healing from violence because I was attacked and raped in my 20s. Much of this book comes from my healing following that event. I made a lot of mistakes along the path of healing as well, and this book also comes from what those mistakes taught me. These experiences, plus my training as a coach, my preparation and ordination as a Gnostic priest, my reflections, and my many teachers have given me insight into how one gets through these deeply challenging times.

This book is for people who have faced violence and who feel ready to heal from the damage that was done to them. Specifically this book is for those who have already survived the violence. It is for those for whom the violence itself has ended.

I realize many people, sadly, live with ongoing violence as a fact in their lives. Healing can still happen for those people, but the path to healing is different from what I describe here. Before healing can truly begin, one needs to be safe. Victims of ongoing violence first need to summon the courage to leave the predicament in which they feel trapped.

If you are still facing recurring physical or emotional violence, I strongly urge you to contact help—a crisis center, a shelter, a domestic abuse hotline—for the support you need to get out and get yourself safe. Appendix B lists some of these resources for you.

Other experiences of violence come in war or political turmoil and torture. I do not pretend to know about the special healing needs of people with those experiences, though I think much of what I have written may be applicable. Again, if this is you, I urge you to seek help specifically focused on the kind of violence you have faced. Appendix B also lists resources for you.

If, however, you have already survived either a single violent event—an assault, a rape, or an attack—or have survived an extended period of repeated violence, this book is for you. Whether what happened to you was recent or ended a long time ago, healing is now a part of your life, and, again, this book is for you. If you think you have pretty much healed from a violent experience but have a vague, nagging feeling that something is not quite right, this book is also for you.

Beyond anything I offer, I urge you to learn to listen to your own inner guidance. There is a wise healing voice within you, as there is within each of us. I will help you find that voice in you, and discover how to trust and follow it.

If you read something that seems helpful, try it. If you read something that seems silly or weird, consider trying it anyway. If you read something that just feels wrong to you, let it go and ignore it. Maybe it will be useful later and maybe it is just not for you. Some of what I offer here is universal and will be of help to you. Trust yourself to know what fits for you.

Throughout the book, I frequently use the pronoun "she" instead of the more awkward phrase "he or she." Sometimes I use "she or he." The majority of people who suffer the sort of violence I am discussing are women. My use of "she" merely makes the book easier to read. I do not at all mean to imply that men are not beaten, raped, or attacked. They are, sadly, and their struggle is every bit as deep and serious as that of women. In the same way, not all perpetrators are men. Women can and do commit terrible acts of violence. I have sometimes used the pronoun "he" referring to a perpetrator for reading ease only.

Surviving violence is like walking in a dark wood: You cannot see very far in front of you. You cannot see where the woods end or how you will get out. You experience fear, disorientation, and the temptation to just give up. I have walked there before you and am dropping these breadcrumbs for you. May they lead you back to the sunshine of knowing who you are and fully being you again.

Introduction

To heal from violence, we have to talk about the dark side of life. Most people avoid talking about the dark, and there is nothing wrong with that. However, when you are the victim of violence, you no longer have that choice. You have been forced into a very frightening darkness. No one can force you to stay there or prevent your coming back to the light. You will, however, first need to be willing to confront the dark, to talk about it, and to want healing so much you will do anything and face everything necessary in order to heal.

In Chapter 1, I share the story of my encounter with violent rape and some of its aftermath. You do not need to read Chapter 1 to use this book, so if you prefer, feel free to skip to Chapter 2, an overview of violence. Briefly, I was raped at knifepoint by a stranger, in my own home, in the middle of the night. My life was turned upside down in just three hours. I knew then and know now that violence changed the whole trajectory of my life. I did not become the person I was on my way to becoming before I was attacked. I could no longer ever be that person. I became instead the person I am, and the journey of my survival and healing is now a very big part of who I am.

If you have survived and are reading this book, you probably already know violence has also upended your life. However you encountered violence—whether a sudden attack or a series of assaults over a long period of time—much of the effect is the same. Maybe you endured a beating, or a rape, or being held hostage, or long-term verbal and psychological abuse. Maybe you suffered violence on many occasions over many years. Any acts done to you in which the doer intended to cause you harm and to exert power over you, or to significantly diminish you, are violence.

Once the violence has ended and you have survived, questions arise. The physical violence may be over and physical injuries may have healed on the outside, but your inside is another matter. You probably still hurt inside, have nightmares, feel fear, doubt yourself, and can easily be overwhelmed. As the hours, days, and weeks pass, your mind may be asking: *Will this ever end? How do I get through this? How do I deal with all this fear/anger/pain/grief? What if I can't stand this? What will happen to me? Why me? Why this? Will I EVER be happy again? Will I ever really be ME again?*

Those are the questions that filled my mind. Finding the answers has taken years—decades, actually. For the most part now, I have answered them. To skip to the bottom line: Yes, it will end; yes, you can get through this; yes, you can stand it; yes, you will be happy again; no, there may not be a reason; and yes, you still are you and you will feel like you again. Right now, do not worry whether you fully believe all that or not. Choose the path of healing and you will get there.

Some other reactions may be familiar to you. I absolutely did not want to be inspired or cheered up. I lived in California at the time, and I wanted none of the New Age-y empty sayings in vogue then. I did not want any form of "happy talk," and anything sounding like a platitude made me want to smash something. What I was going through was big and ugly, painful and frightening. I just wanted all the pain, all the fear, all the grief, and the tight knot inside me to *go away!*

Everything in me also wanted to say, "I'm fine. Leave me alone!" and somehow make it be as if rape had never happened. There were times when I could not stand the turmoil of my feelings so I tried to numb myself—with one substance or another. Dulling the intensity with busy-ness and fantasies only allowed me to avoid living my life mindfully. Numbing did not bring healing.

I wanted at the very least to break a lot of rules. Ordinary life seemed shallow and bland compared to the chaos inside me. I was not even sure I wanted to go back to who I had been.

What I really want you to know is you can get through the crisis and heal even if you do not feel inspired or particularly uplifted right now. I didn't either at first. This book may or may not inspire you or cheer you up. If you intend to heal and are even beginning to commit to healing, you have what you need. Remember you are not as alone as you might sometimes feel. Many survivors who have found healing felt exactly what you are feeling.

Four truths

There are four big truths I want to convey about healing from violence and working your way back to a life you love. Glance back at these when you get discouraged.

First, healing is possible. You *can* be you again, though it will not be quite the same as you were before you survived violence. You will be a wiser, stronger you. Even though you may think many times you cannot ever get through your experience and your memories, I am here to tell you that you can.

You *can* be you again.

Second, it will take time. It will probably take more time than you hope. However, it will also probably take less time than you fear. Along with time, it will take a certain amount of work. This will not be the kind of work we usually think of when we hear the word "work." It will take inner work: awareness, self-compassion, self-nurturing, insight, patience, commitment, and a certain amount of discipline. Ultimately it will take letting go. This book is about all of those.

It will probably take more time than you hope. However, it will also probably take less time than you fear.

Third, you are much more than what happened to you. Though there may be times when you feel as if your entire life has been taken over by your experience, the truth is it has not. You are always more than your emotions, memories, or experiences. No matter how horrible the violence committed against you, there is a deep part of you that is not and can never be harmed. This book is about helping you reconnect to that deeper part and to all the parts of your full self.

No matter how horrible the violence committed against you, there is a deep part of you that is not and can never be harmed.

Fourth, healing is a deliberate choice, always open to you. You must choose healing consciously. Sometimes you may need to reaffirm your choice to heal every day, even every hour. You may get tired or discouraged. You may feel worn down and bewildered sometimes, and those feelings are normal and expected. Choose to heal anyway. If you find you are saying to yourself, "I can't," consider whether you might really be saying, "I won't." If so, recommit to your choice to heal instead. This book is about ways to renew your commitment to healing.

Sometimes you may need to reaffirm your choice to heal every day, even every hour.

The phases of healing

The aftermath of violence, and the process of healing, consists of three main phases. First come shock and crisis. When you have experienced a single attack, shock is the period of disbelief and confusion immediately following. Part of you knows what happened but another part of you refuses to know it. The whole world feels altered and threatening.

When you have experienced a long period of repeated violence and finally leave, shock still comes just from having a new reality. Your life will have changed radically—in mundane ways, such as where you live and how you spend your days, and in profound new ways of thinking of yourself. Relief often does not come right away.

The second phase, the healing itself, is longer. You slowly integrate your experience into your general sense of who you are and how the world is. At times, you may try to escape and numb your feelings, as I did (not a good idea). At other times, you "take the bull by the horns," so to speak, and actively pursue your healing—through your own actions and with the help of others. You develop insights and new wisdom, adding to all aspects of your life.

Finally, there is a third phase I think of as letting go, of simply being done with what happened to you and making peace within yourself. In the third phase, you do not forget what happened, but the memory of violence is no longer at the center of your awareness.

Healing strategies

I offer you five general strategies that ultimately helped me heal.

• The first two—**caring for your body and mind** and **using words as instruments of healing**—are covered in Chapter 3 and Chapter 4. These strategies are for the first two phases, and are essential for the period of shock and crisis.

• The second two—**getting help** and **caring for your spiritual self**—are covered in Chapter 5 and Chapter 6. These are strategies you can begin in the first phase as well, but they are at the heart of the second healing phase.

• The fifth strategy, covered in Chapter 7, follows when you have integrated the first four strategies. **Letting go** is when you are ready to no longer be defined by or centered around the violence that happened to you.

Jumping to the letting go strategy will not work without all the effort you put forth with the first four strategies. I know because, like many things in this book, I tried most of what does not work. I tried to go straight to having my ordeal be finished. The fact is your experience simply will not let go of you until the time is right and you have done the second-phase work of healing. Save Chapter 7 to read when you get there, or read it now and let it give you hope to sustain you through darker and harder times.

Finally in Chapter 8 I include some thoughts for the partners, spouses, family, and friends of those who have been the victims of violence.

Your loved ones can find it very tough to respond to you after you have faced violence. Something different happened to them when violence happened to you, but their experience and their process of recovery will not be like yours. My hope is Chapter 8 can give your loved ones some guidance and assurance that what they are going through is normal and point them toward resources to help them.

Welcome to the beginning of the most important journey of your life: healing from violence!

1

How I Know What I Know

There will probably be aspects of my experience that seem not as bad as what you experienced or that seem worse. I offer it here not for comparison but so you will know which parts of your own experience I also know about from my own.

Encounters with violence cannot be compared. They are all big and they all change the lives of those who face them. Here was mine.

~ ~ ~ ~

In 1973 my life as a single woman and business manager of a children's clinic was ordered and predictable even if it was a little boring. The Saturday evening before Palm Sunday, I had friends who had recently moved back to California from New York City over for dinner. They told the story of how they had been mugged on a Manhattan street and how the husband had seized the mugger's knife by the blade in order to get away. His hand had been cut as he grabbed the knife, but after he did, he and his wife were able to run to safety. I listened intently to their story, said goodnight to them, and went to bed and to sleep.

I awoke a few hours later with a man's hand in a surgical glove over my mouth and a knife blade pressed in the palm of my hand. My brain was confused, as I wondered how my friends' story was somehow happening to me. At first, I assumed I was dreaming. I did not think that for very long, however. I thrashed my body and hit around me with my hand. I quickly felt the rapist's all-too-physical presence.

As soon as I was conscious, he took his hand away from my mouth and instead grabbed my wrist. "Who are you?" I said, and "What do you want?" Then his voice: "I'm the man with a knife at your throat and you know what I want" as he shoved his hand between my legs. My logical brain wondered briefly why he had said "at your throat" when the knife was clearly in my hand. Then I was pulled back to the danger when I smelled blood—my own.

My body became very cold, and the muscles at the base of my abdomen tightened hard. They would remain like that for nearly 10 years. My stomach and intestines twisted and cramped, and I could only breathe shallowly.

My thinking raced from one useless thought to another. I thought about how I might somehow push him out, but realized I probably wouldn't have the strength. I thought about running, but my bed was in a corner and he was between me and the door. I thought about fighting, but I kept feeling the knife. I thought about dying and wondered if this was going to be the last hour of my life. I even thought about how I could deceive him, lie to him, trick him into leaving or going somewhere else, but I had no idea how I could do that.

I did nothing; I did not move. I sat in the dark, smelling the saltiness of blood, the sourness of latex in the surgical gloves he wore, and the odd sweetness of something like patchouli oil he had on him. I kept my hands where I could feel both of his rubbery hands so I could at least anticipate his moves and keep track of the knife in the dark.

I sat like that for three hours, on my bed, my back against one wall, gripping the rapist's wrists. He said he wouldn't hurt me unless I tried to use the phone or turn on a light. I later learned that before he had entered my home and jumped on my bed, he had already dismantled the phone box outside and cut my electricity. My clocks had stopped at 3:15 a.m.

For reasons I did not quite understand at the time, I talked to the rapist about how cruel God must be to put both him and me in such a terrible situation. It seemed to me I could read his mind and knew he was feeling alienated from any God he had ever known. He picked up my words and talked at some length about his anger at God. That anger was, in fact, on his mind. I tried to create some sort of sympathy toward me, some sort of humanity, in the situation. Part of me hoped I could talk him down, talk him out of it, talk him into leaving. Part of me desperately hoped I wasn't as powerless as I feared and actually was.

As the sky began to get light, he told me I was becoming more relaxed and was therefore more dangerous to him. True, I no longer felt as if I could vomit at any moment and I was breathing regularly again. "Relaxed," however, was not the right word to describe me. The terror inside had not diminished. He would not leave, clutched my wrist tighter, and pressed the blade of his knife against my hand again. At that moment, I realized there was no way to get him out of my house until he had completed his crime. I gave up inside and said, "So do it."

I have no need to describe exactly what he did. I felt violated, humiliated, and repulsed every moment. When he finished, he said my first name, and in a way, hearing that was the worst. When I heard my name spoken with mock respect, my fear multiplied. "Poor Patricia." I frantically asked myself how he could possibly know my name. Did I know him from somewhere? Had he broken into my house before? Had he read my mail in the mailbox? Had I encountered him at work, at a store, at a class—where? I began sweating with chills again. I again wanted to vomit.

He announced he was going to leave before light so I would not be able to identify him. Maybe I didn't know him, I thought. So how did he know my name? As he walked to my front door, which I could see from my bed, he told me he would come back and kill me if I called the police. I believed him. He had that knife, and in the increasing light, I could see the dark splotches of blood on my sheets. I memorized what I could of his height and face as he turned back before he left. At that moment, I could not and did not trust he was actually leaving.

I sat for at least 10 minutes wondering if he would suddenly spring out at me. Too many movie images. Eventually I reached for the switch on my bedside lamp, but no light came on. There was my clock, stopped at 3:15 a.m., but now it was already dawn. I stretched to get the phone, lifted the receiver, and heard only silence. I sucked in my breath as I realized I was more completely alone than I had thought. I knew I had to get out and get away.

I dressed and looked out every window. I could not see him, but of course I thought he could have been hiding anywhere. The sun was nearly up. It was 6:20 a.m. according to my watch. I ran for my car parked just outside my front door.

I turned the key in the ignition and tried to look in all directions at once. I saw no one. I backed the car out the driveway. A block away I realized it was over—I had made it—and I tried to cry. I could not. In the dim early morning light, all I could think was "Now what? Where do I go? What do I do? Will I ever be me again?"

~ ~ ~

I went to a friend's house and pounded my fists on her door though it was 6:30 in the morning. That was when I saw how bloody my right hand was. She let me in and went to call the police. I stopped her because I was terrified of the rapist's warning. All I could do—all I wanted to do—was sit with my friend, tell the story over and over, then be quiet and hope eventually I would be able to cry. I wanted my mind to stop, but it could not stop. I wanted the ordeal to end, but it could not end for many days, then weeks, then years.

2

About Violence

The Center for Disease Control and Prevention reports that over 12 million men and women experience violence from their intimate partners in the U.S. every year. This translates to 24 people per minute. The American Psychological Association says 3 or more U.S. women are murdered by their husbands or boyfriends each day. These numbers do not include the violence of war or civil disturbance nor do they include violence committed by strangers. With numbers like those, the unfortunate truth is most of us will either face violence ourselves or will know someone who has.

Violence is entirely the fault of the perpetrator, 100% of the time.

I once gave a talk to a women's club about rape prevention. The audience consisted of about 50 women. At the beginning of my talk, I asked how many had either experienced rape or experienced attempted rape themselves, or who personally knew someone who had. As I watched about 80 percent raise their hands, I also noticed two or three women begin to cry. I was still only a few years into recovering from rape myself at the time. I was strangely comforted by such direct evidence of the widespread impact of rape and of the lasting and painful nature of its effects. People who survive violence feel isolated, not because violence only happens to a few but because even though it happens to so many, it has so often been kept quiet and misunderstood.

About violence

Violence is all about power, control, and doing harm. Healing from violence is about reclaiming your power and control. Healing is also about actively choosing to heal and continually reaffirming that choice. Although healing is not always easy, every day really does offer new healing opportunities.

Here is the thing about violence: It hurts you. In fact, I define it as any act in which the intention is to do harm and exert forced control over another. Willful negligence can also be violent and cause harm. Negligence and disregard for the well-being of others arise out of bias, bigotry, racism, ignorance, and capitulating to mob-think, or out of serving unjust institutions of power. The news is filled with examples of violence, overt and covert. We hear about sports figures abusing their partners and college women being raped. We also hear about homeless men dying in harsh Northern winters when they have no place to escape the cold and impoverished women unable to feed their children adequately.

One particular manifestation of violence—date rape—has begun capturing headlines recently. Date rape is nothing new, sadly, but awareness of date rape and the "rape culture" that supports it are finally growing. Date rape is insidious because the rapist by definition is someone known to the survivor. The lines of criminality and responsibility can feel blurred. A survivor may be especially concerned, wondering whether she or he did something to invite an attack or was at least somehow negligent in not protecting herself or himself well enough.

With the advent of smartphones and social media, an especially vicious new form of emotional and physical violence has emerged. Acts of violence, particularly rape, are videoed and posted online, allowing even more people to watch and be "entertained" by the horror, including people known to the survivor, and creating more continuing anguish and humiliation for the survivor.

It does not matter what you did, what you wore, what you said, where you went, or what you drank.

Remember this truth if you are a survivor: *Violence is not your fault— could not be your fault—not ever.* It does not matter what you did, what you wore, what you said, where you went, or what you drank. Violence committed against you is not your fault. No one ever asks to be victimized or invites violence. Violence is entirely the fault of the perpetrator, 100% of the time. Even if you did not exercise your best judgment at some point, you did not ask for violence, and it simply cannot be your fault it happened.

The harm of violence may be primarily physical or emotional or, as is often the case, both. Not all the harm you have suffered will show on the outside. You may feel crushed or dehumanized, terrified or desperate, but no one can just look at you and see all that. Whatever form the harm takes, it affects you deeply. When you are made the victim of violence you become temporarily powerless, and your loss of control can be devastating. When you are victimized, you lose a level of innocence and naivete. You no longer trust the world in the same way.

Such deep losses necessarily produce a big reaction. You cannot help it. Life is not what you always thought it was. Still, your life is not something you can ignore, no matter how hard you try or how much you may want to ignore it. Your sense of safety and your entire worldview, for that matter, are altered or destroyed. You may be unsure how you will live in a world now revealed to have so much danger in it.

In a culture where violence is pervasive and commonplace, absolutely no one can be sure it won't happen to them.

Here is another thing about violence: It can and does happen to every kind of person. Violence does not discriminate or discern among people. Money and status do not protect anyone from it. People of all races and both genders encounter violence. Certain forms of violence may be more prevalent among some groups than others, but every group faces it. Geography, religion, education—none protect anyone from violence, either. In the United States, we live in a violent culture that tolerates, accepts, encourages, rewards, and horrifyingly even enjoys watching, violence. We use the images of violence as a basis for entertainment—in movies, on TV, in video games, in books. In a culture where violence is pervasive and commonplace, absolutely no one can be sure it won't happen to them.

When you are violently attacked, other issues in you may also surface. All the emotional pain you have ever felt, for whatever reason, can suddenly be right there in front of you. That is what happened to me. All your beliefs about people and God may be deeply challenged. Again, that is what happened to me. When you have felt the impact of someone else's intention to harm you, you know you will never be able to forget how that intention felt. The physical harm you experienced—the cuts, bruises, broken bones, injured organs, lost blood—may actually be easier and less lasting than the harm done to your emotions and your soul.

To heal after violence, I believe you must, over time and with support, fully face all of what happened to you, and consciously take back control and responsibility for your own life. By looking deep within yourself, you will find the resources to heal. I believe you must address your mental and emotional needs as well as your physical needs, and ultimately you must address your spiritual needs as well. This book can show you how to move in that direction.

Violence comes in many forms

Many forms of violence exist and differing cultural norms surround each.

The first thing we tend to think of when we think of violence is physical harm: beating, hitting, punching, slapping, cutting, stabbing, choking, burning, even shooting. We think of attempted murder, rape, assault, mugging, domestic abuse, war. We think of broken bones, bruises, cuts, gunshot wounds, and damaged vital organs. Maybe we think of single attacks or maybe we think of sustained violence in abusive relationships, kidnapping, or combat. We may think of more localized violent conflict such as gang wars and neighborhood conflict. Violence is all of those things, but it is also more.

Anything intended to do harm and/or exert forced control over another is violence.

There is also violence that targets emotional well-being. Bullying is emotional violence. So are repeated harsh put-downs and insults. Acts of terrorism have an impact on whole societies, not just on those who experience them physically. Terrorism is emotional violence. Harassment and stalking are emotional violence. All forms of deliberate intimidation are emotional violence. Uncontrolled verbal expressions of rage are violence. *Anything* intended to do harm and/or exert forced control over another is violence.

What lies beneath

People do not generally like to think about violence. They may be comfortable seeing it in entertainment or reading about it from a safe distance in the news, but they do not like to think seriously about how close it always is. They particularly do not like to recognize their own personal vulnerability to violence. When you have been victimized, you are a walking reminder of what people don't want to know, and some will avoid you because of it.

Many people I knew wanted quite badly to believe what happened to me could not happen to them. They often searched for ways I was to blame. They wanted to identify things I had done that they thought they would never do. Those things could then allow them to think they knew why this thing had happened to me but would never happen to them. People latched on to just about anything. I had left my window open at night. I had once worn shorts to the store. I had long hair.

The need to blame victims is widespread and common.

I now believe this need to blame victims is widespread and common. It may even be somewhat understandable, but it nevertheless causes a great deal of emotional pain. I understand we all want to avoid facing our vulnerability in this world. Vulnerability makes everyone uncomfortable. You, however, having survived violence, cannot help but face yours. Vulnerability is now in the middle of your everyday awareness.

We need a certain level of denial in order to live in a world we know to be dangerous. If we were to focus all the time on the danger of violence, we would soon become paralyzed and unable to live our lives. We simply need denial in order to function. When violence happens to someone we know, our denial is threatened. Unconsciously, we try to re-establish our denial. If we can convince ourselves we are not like the person who was victimized in some important aspect, we can assure ourselves we are safer than we actually are. The need for denial is a powerful reason society blames the victim. Having survived violence, you are unfortunately very likely to encounter this sort of blame.

Many of us share also a subconscious and irrational fear that another person's suffering might be contagious. We seem to think simply avoiding the person is easier and safer, even if she or he is a close friend or relative. The survivor's need for comforting or support gets lost in our fear. Understanding this kind of fear saddens me. I was deeply hurt by such fear in others following my rape, and you may be, too. The fear and the pain, however, are real and sadly, are common.

Even deeper than the vulnerability people do not want to think about, there is something harder to face: People do not want to think about their own capacity for perpetrating violence. This is a tough one, since most of us believe we are peaceful people who would never commit acts of violence. True, perhaps, but I believe we harbor a delusion if we think we do not have within us the capacity to commit violence.

Psychiatrist Carl Jung called the hidden and unwanted part of ourselves our "shadow" and explained how aspects of ourselves that we cannot tolerate consciously become hidden from our awareness. Whether we are aware of them or not, those aspects nonetheless are still within us.

I learned about part of my own shadow when the man who raped me was finally arrested after eight years. I thought of myself as a person who thoroughly abhorred violence. Consciously that was true. At the lineup to identify him, I walked up close to the glass separating me from the five similar-looking men. I heard each man say the words I had heard the night I was raped. As I heard the actual rapist say them, something snapped in me. Every bit of my being wanted to smash the glass and use the shards to cut him to pieces, gouge out his eyes, slit his throat, eviscerate him, castrate him. I could feel a violent longing not only in my mind, but physically in my muscles, in my belly, and in my hands. I really wanted to kill, right there, right then.

I knew with certainty and with horror I had within me the capacity for murder. I was appalled and quite shaken. My self-image was altered forever. I now think the awareness of this shadow part of me was an important part of my healing into greater consciousness. I consciously choose not to indulge that part of myself by acting on it ever, but now I know it is there.

Many people will do anything, including blaming survivors, to sustain their beliefs about themselves and protect their illusions.

Many people deeply do not want to know the violence within themselves. Many people will do anything, including blaming survivors, to sustain their beliefs about themselves and protect their illusions.

Paradoxically, knowing the shadow part of myself has made me more compassionate for people who cannot face their own shadows. Even though it is clearly unfair, you need to be prepared to encounter this kind of blaming after you have survived violence. Try to remember the blaming really is not about you at all.

Media make us impatient

In recent decades, violence has been portrayed in the entertainment media more and more realistically and graphically. On any night, you can see and hear scenes of rape, assault, gun fighting, verbal abuse, even murder. If healing is portrayed at all and the victim is not simply dead, discarded, or dropped from the storyline, healing will take place within an hour or two and no more than a few weeks.

Perhaps an episode or two will show the survivor in the process of healing (see old episodes of *Private Practice* and *The Sopranos*), but within a month the story will get old and the writers will focus on a new storyline. If the survivor is a main character, she or he will go back to being the same person she or he was when the series started. She may mention what happened to her a few times, but the long-term experience of healing will not be shown. If not a main character, he or she will likely fade away and be written out. The message is clear: You only get so much time to heal, and that is it. We do not have patience for more.

The real world is different. Real healing takes place over months and years. Your healing will take a long time. You will probably subconsciously want it to end as fast as it does in the movies, but it will not. Taking time does not mean anything is wrong with you. Entertainment by its nature presents quick resolutions so new plots can be introduced. Your life is not like that. Your life will take what it takes.

Healing happens on its own timetable.

Healing happens on its own timetable, different for every survivor. How you heal is a function of your history, your personality, your resources, your beliefs, the depth of injury you sustained, your support network, your physical well-being, and your ability to secure safety and help for yourself.

The emotions following violence

Facing violence brings up powerful emotions. Even if you work hard to suppress them, the emotions will be there. They simply have to be dealt with, and much of this book talks about how to deal with them.

Fear can feel as if it will never go away.
Be gentle wth yourself. It will not last forever.

Two major feelings that arise are fear and anger. It is profoundly frightening to have someone else exert power over you, hurt you with malicious intent, and violate your space and even your body. The fear can feel as if it will never go away and never be diminished, even after you have made it to safety. Images may appear in your imagination whenever you are quiet. You may have nightmares. You may find yourself feeling anxious even when you are not conscious of any imagery at all. I experienced all of those for quite a while. Be gentle with yourself and know the feelings are natural, are normal, and will not last forever.

How could there not be anger when you have been diminished and subjugated by another person?

Anger comes early for some people and much later for others, but it frequently follows a violent assault. How could there not be anger when you have been diminished and subjugated by another person? Part of what determines the amount of anger you feel is your basic personality and what you believe about anger. If you are not accustomed to expressing anger, you may not feel it after violence, either, or you may feel it much later. If anger comes easily to you, you are more likely to feel it early on.

Your anger and how you express it can also be determined by what happens after the attack. When the support you receive is caring and wise, and the professionals you must encounter are compassionate and competent, your anger may be lessened or soothed. On the other hand, if you feel treated unfairly and harshly by others, whether police, medical personnel, or friends, your anger may be compounded. Again, be gentle with yourself. Anger, like fear, is common.

Anger may even be quite healthy. When you get back in touch with your personal power and realize how deeply it has been violated, anger is a natural response. Anger coming from your power can be an effective part of your healing. You can channel anger into constructive action, particularly action benefitting others.

I became active in supporting a change in the statute of limitations for serial rape so more cases could be brought to trial. A client of mine volunteered as an advocate for other survivors. An expression of anger can be either constructive or destructive. You always have the choice. Choose the constructive path of healing.

Grief is a third big emotion after violence. I did not recognize this one for a long time. I simply felt immense sadness and cried spontaneously even when I was not able to point to anything in the moment to account for it. I realized eventually I was grieving for the future life I had thought I was going to have and had now lost. I was grieving because all of my future would now have the memory of rape in it. I was actually grieving for my own lost innocence and naivete. Grief lasted longer for me than either my fear or my anger. If you feel grief, know again you are not alone, and it, too, is normal.

Your powerful emotions after violence are not contagious, and you do not need to protect anyone else from them.

Your powerful emotions after violence are not contagious, and you do not need to protect anyone else from them. It is important to let yourself feel what is true for you. Not everyone around you will be able to walk through it with you, unfortunately. Never worry, however, that your feelings are somehow going to hurt someone else.

Recognize the limitations of those in your life who may have limitations. And do your best not to use their limitations or judgments to put yourself down or suppress your truth. Their stuff is their stuff, and you need not take it on. Later in this book you will read about how to find the help and support you need.

The one "emotion" I want to warn you about is shame. I actually do not believe shame is a real emotion in the same sense fear, anger, and grief are emotions. I truly believe shame is something you have within your power to stop. Shame, to my mind, is often a second-level reaction to the strength of other emotions when you perceive those emotions to be "too much." Shame has its roots in the cultural images of strength and pseudo-healing pushed on to us. It is a reaction to someone else's idea of how you should feel or should have acted. Finally, it is an aftereffect of the humiliation and extreme vulnerability you experienced.

It seems to me shame comes fundamentally from believing that, as a survivor, you "should" be, think, or act in a particular way—or you should have done so earlier—while at the same time knowing you did not or cannot. It comes from believing you "should" have been able to avoid or lessen your attack while at the same time being unable to imagine how you could really have done differently.

Here is how it works. Violence diminishes you and overcomes your most fundamental abilities to protect yourself, your home, even your body. You are like everyone else and try to find some way you may have contributed to the violence happening so you will not have to face your real vulnerability. You wonder if you "deserved" violence in some way. At some level, you may feel more in control if you can identify some change you could make to be safer.

Perhaps you feel especially embarrassed by the exact way violence was inflicted on you, so you feel an even stronger need to figure out what you could have done. Maybe you are not reacting as the characters in the movies react to violence. All these concerns give rise to shame. Plus, society is always there, ready to reinforce your shame as a way of blaming and distancing you. No wonder shame causes so much suffering for so many survivors.

Shame is something you have within your power to stop.

I still believe you have the power inside you to stop shame. The problem is with the "should." You will need time and support to change your "should" beliefs. Here, however, is the truth again: You are not—and could not possibly be—to blame for what happened to you. The media are at last beginning to deliver this message. Still, it bears repeating since we need to overcome decades—even centuries—of victim blaming. Violence is *always* the fault of the perpetrator.

The way out of shame is to challenge your own beliefs about how you "should" be or "should" have been. Keep challenging those beliefs until they yield to genuine self-acceptance and compassion. In Chapter 5 you will read about finding the support you need. In Chapter 6 you will learn about acceptance. For now, know that self-love and acceptance are the antidotes to the poison of shame. Both are within your reach.

> **The way out of shame is to challenge your own beliefs about how you "should" be or "should" have been.**

In summary, when you survive violence your entire life is affected. Violence affects you physically, mentally, emotionally, and spiritually. Violence is about power, and your own power has been temporarily taken away. You have been hurt in multiple ways. Violence can and does happen to every kind of person. Our culture still does not give you much support for healing from violence and in many cases actually makes it harder. Powerful emotions inevitably arise from violence; they are normal. No one ever deserves violence—not you, not anyone. You do not deserve blame. People close to you are also affected by what happened to you, but they may not be able to stand by you even if they want to.

The next chapters give you steps you can take on your own to further your own healing.

~ ~ ~ ~

"I was so low and vulnerable that I believed what [people] said....
People heard but they thought I wasn't worth saving
because it was my fault...."
~ Survivor of domestic abuse

"I was looking for someone to name what had happened to me.
Without this naming, I remained alone with a terrible knowledge."
~ Patricia Weaver Francisco,
Telling: A Memoir of Rape and Recovery

3

Take Care: Your Body

After surviving a violent assault, your needs and the demands on you multiply rapidly. You may have serious physical needs in the aftermath of physical injury (cuts, bruises, fractures) that need to be treated and need to heal—or, worse, injuries requiring surgery to repair.

A mountain of new tasks accumulates on your to-do list, it seems, even if you did not want them. You have to engage in things such as talking to police, and filling out crime reports and insurance claims. Dealing with your job is another challenge. You need to consider if you want to take a leave of absence or if you need to negotiate to work part-time for a while. You may need or discover you want to change your housing. Your home may have damage requiring repairs you will have to arrange. I had all of those and more, and they drove me nearly mad during the first weeks.

> At the same time you have to cope with new demands
> you will have quite a bit less energy
> than you are used to having.

At the same time you have to cope with many new demands and unfamiliar things to do, you likely will have quite a bit less energy than you are used to having. You may be struggling with paralyzing levels of fear and anxiety, or immobilizing anger. You may be sleep deprived and exhausted. You will certainly be preoccupied and distracted.

Take care and get care

One of your first priorities must be to seek medical care if you have injuries. Even though your need may be obvious, it can be very difficult to go to a doctor after you have been attacked. You may be afraid to be touched. I experienced that. You may be anxious about telling the story of what happened to you. I was, too. You may feel shame and humiliation. The perpetrators of violence try to make you feel shame and fear, and even after the attack the feelings linger. You may be afraid of being judged somehow, asked whether you "asked for it," or told you should not have "let this happen to you." You have seen how TV and movies reinforce these fears. Whatever the source of your feelings and resistance, when you feel them, you feel them. It does not mean anything is wrong with you.

You must muster the courage to get your body what it needs.

Nobody is entirely rational in the immediate aftermath of a violent attack. You must, however, muster the courage to get your body what it needs. You need professional help to assess and treat any injuries. Perhaps you need a bone set, need stitches or medication, need major surgery, or simply need reassurance that your internal organs are not damaged. You also need to know how you can care for yourself as your body heals.

I went to my doctor alone because that is what worked for me. I am, in many ways, a private person. You may want to take a friend or partner with you when you go for care or follow-up care. The right companion can provide comfort, support, and another set of ears to hear whatever information is given to you. She or he can also reduce your stress by driving you to your doctor visit and minimizing the walking you have to do. You may want to have someone just to lean on or hold onto if the session becomes difficult for you.

If you can, you may find it useful to voice any fears you have to your friend or partner. Stating in words what you are afraid of often clarifies how you can take care of yourself if your fears should materialize. If you go alone, consider telling the medical provider what you fear. A compassionate provider can then take your emotional needs into account as he or she cares for your physical needs.

> ## Courage is about feeling what you really feel and doing what needs to be done anyway.

Most important, let yourself be what you are and do what you feel you need to do. If you need to cry, cry. If you need to be silent, be silent. If you need medications to help with anxiety or sleep, ask for them. If you are angry, be angry. As you know, courage is not about being unafraid or not anxious. Courage is about feeling what you really feel and doing what needs to be done anyway. Simply surviving is courageous, so you already know you have proven your courage.

The early days can be tough

Just after I was raped, I found every hour of my days to be fairly challenging. The challenges did not lighten even a little for several weeks. Do not be surprised if you struggle to get through the days. Some of my clients have talked about sitting at home doing virtually nothing, talking to no one, for days and even weeks. Everything they might have done felt much too challenging. I was shocked when I was barely able to do simple things, such as buying groceries—things that were previously easy for me. I now know such paralysis is more common than one might think.

At work, I could not even dial the phone. I could not explain why I could not do it; I just could not. I would pick up the phone, stare at it, and put it down. Weirdly, I seemed to prefer judging myself for not making the call rather than having *any* routine interaction with the world. Some semi-conscious part of me resisted the world moving forward normally. I felt somehow as if my having been violated meant everyone should stop and gasp indefinitely. Put that way, of course it sounds ridiculous, but the feelings and fear were not at all ridiculous. They were, in fact, quite debilitating and painful.

For a couple of months, I would not go out alone at night, no matter what needed to be done. I imagined I saw the rapist everywhere I went: outside the post office, in the hardware store, across a parking lot. I jumped if I heard footsteps behind me as I walked downtown, even in daylight. I struggled to keep his face in my memory so I could recognize it if I saw him or report it accurately to the police artist if I ever went.

Sleep posed a particular challenge. For a week, I slept at a friend's house while she and another of our friends slept on either side of me on the floor in sleeping bags. That and a few milligrams of Valium allowed me to get a little sleep each night. When I did finally fall asleep, I found it very difficult to wake up. Sleep usually came to me inconveniently during daylight, the time when offices were open and I either had to be at work or needed to be doing other tasks.

I could not eat much and was nauseated most of the time. I could think of little but what had happened and was uninterested in food. I was even unable to use a table knife to cut my food, so friends had to help me. I had to look away from all knives. When a friend took out a carving knife to cut roast beef she had made, I started sobbing and trembling, surprised and unable to stop. I had finally started crying after nearly two weeks. Similar strong emotional reactions would rise up in me unexpectedly and take me over from time to time, making me cry, shake, even scream. The tears came from somewhere deep inside me, beyond my conscious reach.

Violence has a huge impact on every part of you. It really is okay to slow down for a while.

If your early days after violence are like mine were, be especially gentle and forgiving with yourself. Remind yourself you simply cannot immediately go back to being the same competent person you were accustomed to being. Violence has a huge impact on every part of you. It really is okay to slow down for a while.

Your body's basic needs matter now

Your body is under tremendous stress during and after violence. Even if you do not have major physical injuries, you still have the stress. At the most basic level, you need both sleep and excellent nutrition while you may feel as if you do not want either. I wished I could just avoid sleeping altogether since the mere act of closing my eyes made my heart pound faster. I lost my appetite almost completely, so I did not eat or ate only one or two bites a couple of times a day.

It is more important than you might think to do whatever is necessary to get the sleep and food you need. Without them, the stress is worse and a negative spiral starts. Now, when something happens to take away my appetite, I make sure I get nutrient-dense food like energy shakes and I use supplements. In extreme circumstances I use medications to be sure I can sleep.

Exercise also helps relieve stress. I did not do that one either at the time, but I wish I had and I do now. There are good physiological reasons why exercise can help you through the time after an attack. Exercise can also enhance your ability to sleep and improve your appetite for healthy food. The athletic shoe slogan "Just Do It" applies here. Just as with sleep and food, try not to let exercise become just another "should" that starts to feel like a burden. Instead, think of yourself as someone you love who has been seriously hurt and who needs your extra loving care. Give that care to yourself in the form of sleep, food, and exercise.

About numbing out

I fell into a common trap when my feelings of vulnerability, anger, grief, and fear became too much for me. I wanted desperately to stop feeling, just to go numb, to get a break. You may feel similarly, and likely will feel that way more than once. Again I want to tell you what I wish I had done differently in the hope that you will believe me and do better for yourself. My mistakes first, however.

I drank alcohol. Actually, I only drank alcohol on two occasions. I thought I could escape my horrible feelings with alcohol and quickly discovered I could not. Alcohol does not give you any kind of instant happy feelings. After the attack, alcohol did pretty much nothing in my body, leaving my feelings the same. I did not get any kind of "high."

Knowing alcohol is really a depressant and can quickly make everything worse, I stopped right away. I could see the danger of possible alcohol abuse.

The danger I did not see was sugar. Sugar is initially pleasant with a positive effect on brain chemistry. Immediately after I was raped, I stopped eating very much at all and lost 20 pounds rapidly. Once I finally started eating again, I craved the positive effect of sugar. Sugar does not seem dangerous since it is only food. My need for sugar escalated rapidly, however, and my weight along with it. The sweetness seemed to counteract my pain, both metaphorically and chemically, at least for a few minutes each time, sometimes for hours.

There was, however, no end to it. No matter how much sugar I consumed (and some days it was a sickening amount) the emotional pain never stopped. Sugar instead increased my depression, made me start hating myself for giving into it, did considerable harm to my body, and led to my craving more with every day. Within a year, I had developed classic addiction.

You cannot numb the pain. Period. Do not even try.

So here is the rest of the truth: You cannot numb the pain. Period. Do not even try. Stay away from what I call the "numbing agents" in our world. These include alcohol, recreational drugs, sugar, food in general, excessive or compulsive exercise, compulsive sex, gambling, video games, television, cigarettes, and anything else you might do solely to be distracted and escape from your feelings and your life. They will not and cannot take away your pain.

What is more, if you notice you feel compulsive and driven to seek out your chosen numbing agent, you already have less personal power than ever just when you need more. Compulsion and addiction open the door to intense feelings of shame, whether you let yourself feel them or not, and you surely do not need shame after you have faced violence. As you eat more, drink more, smoke more, gamble more, or do more to numb yourself, you are likely also to isolate yourself to keep your behavior hidden. Isolation in turn will increase your emotional and even your spiritual pain. You can find yourself alone, ashamed, terrified of yourself, in denial, and in very deep pain. I did.

This does not mean you never drink, eat, or do anything that could possibly become an addiction. You must, however, stay aware and remain honest with yourself. Notice if you feel compelled to turn to any one substance or activity over and over. When something you do stops giving you pleasure and starts feeling like something you cannot live without, you are in trouble. If you see this pattern in yourself, get help soon. In Chapter 5 you will learn more about how.

To truly heal you must face your reality squarely.

The compulsion to escape your reality is the real problem. To truly heal, however, you just plain must face your reality squarely. In facing a reality that includes violence, you will probably need support and help. All any of the numbing agents can provide at best is momentary escape in exchange for demanding, depleting, and destroying an increasing part of your life.

When you can tough it through your negative emotions, strengthen your positive emotions, nurture your body, mind, and spirit, and face your reality honestly you will get beyond it all faster. You simply have to choose healing over numbing. Without doubt, your negative feelings will have their day, too, as you heal. Whatever you do not or will not feel now, you will surely feel later. Trust me on this one. In short, **numbing out only drags it out.**

Whatever you do not or will not feel now, you will surely feel later.

Safety first, and second, and...

Do whatever it takes for you to feel physically safe enough to heal. Maybe you will decide to move to a shelter, at least temporarily, or to a new home. Maybe you will want to stay with someone else or have someone stay with you for a while. You may need to deal with police or the courts to press charges or get a restraining order to keep yourself safer from the perpetrator.

The National Network to End Domestic Violence, on its website, offers many suggestions about staying safe. See Appendix B for the organization's contact information. Rape crisis centers and some law-enforcement agencies also offer strategies and even classes on keeping yourself safe.

I did several things immediately after I was raped in order to feel physically safe. After my week at a friend's home I found a new place to live and moved. I never again slept in the house where I was attacked. I started getting my mail at a post office box and refused to have my name and street address appear together anywhere. I even convinced the state of California to let me have a P.O. box on my driver's license.

After seven years, I moved out of state. Then, for 10 more years, I would not live anywhere on a ground floor or where my door opened to the outside. I wanted more than one locked door between me and the world. Yes, that was pretty extreme, but I needed those doors to feel safe.

If you cannot change your living quarters readily but you also do not feel safe where you are, there are less-drastic things you can do. Change your locks. Install deadbolt locks or an alarm system. I put in a system that I could arm during the night with a button next to my bed to use to silently summon police if necessary. Some people have put bars on their windows, though I wonder if that might not feel like you are the one inside prison when the perpetrator should be.

If sounds disrupt your sleep too much, consider using a white noise machine, soothing recordings, or ear plugs. If not being able to hear every small sound scares you, however, find ways to reduce any extraneous sounds in your space.

Protect your emotional safety as well. Figure out what upsets you and triggers your feelings of vulnerability or fear. Then simply do not do or be near those things to the extent you can. While avoiding triggers may be easier said than done, it is important to give yourself a good, long break from the things that trigger you.

It is important to give yourself a good, long break from the things that trigger you.

For me, this meant avoiding violent movies, even artistically excellent ones, for more than 10 years. I would not see a movie until someone I trusted had seen it first and could tell me what to expect. Even then, I might decide not to go. That is how I, a serious movie fan who had grown up on the edge of Hollywood, missed all the *Godfather* movies, *The Deerhunter*, and *Platoon*. I still avoid violent movies for the most part but out of my free choice, not out of fear or triggers.

Trust your body and listen to the voice inside you

Your body senses more than you can ever be consciously aware of. You can see this is true. Pay attention the next time you walk into a store or any place with a lot of people. You will feel something right away. The feelings are subtle but they are unmistakable once you learn to recognize them. Does the place feel "safe" or "quiet"? How about "creepy"? Do you feel slightly anxious or very relaxed? Do you feel annoyed, hassled, pressured? How about comfortable, able to calmly get what you came to get? Look around you. Does anything you see make you uneasy?

Your body remembers more than you consciously remember.

Your body also remembers more than you consciously remember. Sometimes the sensations in your body are based on unconscious body memories. Part of your brain remembers everything you have ever experienced. That part of your brain will do whatever it can to keep you safe if you encounter a situation reminding it of an earlier danger. You will get a alarm signal from your body. Pay attention! You might get on a bus and sense such a feeling. You may be walking along the street or in a store, and sense something or someone behind you. You may hear a noise at night that you cannot immediately identify. You might not like the looks of a parking lot and not know why. You may walk into an apparently innocuous place (a movie theater, a party, a coffee shop, a store) and be hit with a deep uneasiness.

Here is the thing: If you feel it, it is real for you. Maybe there is present danger nearby and maybe not. That does not matter. If you *feel* in danger or apprehensive, you need to act. You do not have to spend time in any place that feels uncomfortable. You have a right to be safe and to make whatever changes you can in order to feel safe. Your safety is far more important than avoiding embarrassment.

Here are some ways survivors have described the subtle danger signals that arise: a hard lump or "knot" in the belly, tight muscles on the pelvic floor, a wave of energy feeling cold and vaguely electric, a faster heart rate, shallow breathing, chills in the arms or shoulders. Become conscious of what your body feels. Your body has deep wisdom within it and responds to what is real whether you are aware or not. I once saw in a photograph that I had made a fist I did not remember making. At the time the picture was taken, I had not had any awareness of feeling emotionally unsafe. My hand knew it, though.

Your body has deep wisdom within it and responds to what is real whether you are aware or not.

When you feel alarm, however small, *do something* to change your situation.

What gets in the way of trusting your body

One big thing that often stands in the way of trusting your body's signals is a fear of feeling foolish or looking silly. You may wonder if you are just "jumpy" and "overreacting," so you ignore the sensations. Perpetrators rely on our reluctance to seem irrational or break social rules in order to trap us into dangerous situations. If you just got on a bus and do not feel quite right, you may resist the idea of immediately getting right back off the bus since everyone on the bus might stare at you. You may feel embarrassed crossing the street in the middle of a block because you do not like the feeling you get from the person walking behind you. *Do it anyway.* Listen to your body.

Perpetrators rely on our reluctance to seem irrational or break social rules in order to trap us into dangerous situations.

Another obstacle to acting on your body's signals can be that you have an agenda and do not want to be waylaid. You may need something in a store or really want to see a particular movie, and you do not want to make a scene or be inconvenienced by walking out. You want to get what you came to the store to get, knowing you are just a few feet away from it down the aisle in front of you. You do not want to go across town. You do not want to leave, but you feel that little alarm going off inside you. *Leave anyway.* Listen to your body.

It takes more courage to listen to your body and act on its signals than it does to exhibit bravado.

A third obstacle is pride. Pride really got in my way. You want to be "strong" and you do not want to feel fear, so you tell yourself you aren't feeling it even when you are. You have a self-image you are trying to maintain, probably created before you faced violence, and you do not want to "give in" to the knot or the lump or the chill. You want to walk confidently with your head held high to show yourself you are still the same person. But you are not the exact same person. You are no longer naive; you are a survivor. It is okay—in fact it is imperative—that you actually let yourself feel what you feel. If you are not strong in the way you used to think of as strong, know that you are actually stronger. It takes more courage to listen to your body and act on its signals than it does to exhibit bravado. *Do it.* Listen to your body.

Take it easy, make it easy

Healing from violence takes a great deal of energy. Though you may easily forget, the truth is that half or more of you is always engaged in doing the healing. The entire rest of your life only gets, at best, half of you. As a result, you now have limits in your regular life that you did not have before you faced violence. For example, you may find you cannot balance a checkbook when you know perfectly well you used to be able to do it. Maybe you cannot remember things you know you know: your friend's phone number, your online or smartphone passwords, the date you are supposed to go to the dentist. Stress impairs your memory significantly. Do not beat yourself up over it.

Stress impairs your memory significantly. Do not beat yourself up over it.

This is no time to be superwoman or superman. From the perspective of where you are at the beginning of your healing, even your old self is a sort of superwoman or superman. Do your best to accept your temporary limitations. Give yourself a break by doing two things:

Do less. Take some time off or scale back your work responsibilities for a while if you can. Delegate some of your responsibilities to co-workers. *Do not* start new projects, make new investments, make major purchases, even start new relationships for a while. If you're like me, you will want to disrupt your life and do a lot of new things—as a distraction and because the energy of newness can be exhilarating. Trust me on this one, too. Taking on anything major and new is a mistake. The distraction and exhilaration are short-lived. You will instead soon have another set of responsibilities that also feel overwhelming.

Use your time and energy to keep to a soothing routine that includes caring for yourself with food, sleep, and exercise. A certain amount of superficial boredom is fine while you are healing. The work of healing goes on beneath the surface and really needs a high percentage of your energy so the process can go on. Let it be so.

Use tools. There are countless tools available to help compensate for your diminished energy and memory. You can put reminders on your phone or computer for anything you need to remember to do. You can set multiple reminders for each event so you do not have to worry if you are unable to attend to the first reminder when it comes up. You can use a calendar, whether electronic or paper, to keep track of appointments, birthdays, meetings, even movies or TV shows you want to be sure to see.

You can use sticky notes (again, electronic or paper) wherever you want to be reminded to do something or think about something. You can stick them on your bathroom mirror, the steering wheel of your car, your closet door, your refrigerator—anywhere. You can use them to keep a mantra (see the next chapter) in the front of your mind. Just keep moving them so they do not become invisible out of habit. They will help relieve your feelings of being overwhelmed. You will not be afraid of forgetting something when you have put it on a note or calendar.

I found having a master list always with me was essential for the first few weeks. On it I kept all the phone numbers of people I needed to keep informed (friends, police investigators, doctors' offices), insurance claim numbers, case file numbers, even my car's license plate number. If anyone asked me to do something or go somewhere or gave me a good bit of advice, on to the list it went. Smartphones make keeping a list even easier. After a month or so, I dropped the list, but it was of great value during the first busy and demanding days.

Cultivate a relationship with yourself

When your body, and with it your psyche, has been hurt, as it has when you are subjected to violence, it can be quite difficult to connect back to it. Such body alienation is, in my opinion, one of the more challenging aspects of violence's aftermath. Based on my own experience and the stories I have heard from clients, I believe we instinctively separate ourselves psychologically or energetically from our bodies when our body is being harmed. This is a function of basic self-protection. We withdraw our awareness from the unthinkable, maybe unbearable, experience our body is having. If we did not, we fear we might go mad from the sheer enormity of the horror or pain. We survive, but the price is high.

When the experience has ended, reconnecting with your body can be tough.

When the experience has ended, reconnecting with your body can be tough. On the simplest level, you may still have physical pain or injuries. More importantly, you may be unwilling to feel the emotions in your body: anxiety, humiliation, overwhelm, terror, or any of a number of other emotions. You may feel your mind is a safer place to be than your body. Believe me, it is not. Your mind and spirit need your body, and your body needs your mind and spirit. All three have to heal together, for they are all you.

The exercises at the end of this chapter suggest some simple ways to reconnect with your body. You can also use your body to do something you find valuable. For a musician, this might mean mastering a piece you love. For an artist, it may mean creating a painting or sculpture. It may mean completing a physical challenge such as climbing a rock or mountain (if you already know how!) or even riding a bike or rowing a canoe, snorkeling, or dancing. I did some of those and can attest that each helped in a different way. Stay mindful, however, of your temporary energy limitations.

One rather unusual step that helped me a great deal was posing for an artist. I sat for her on the 30th anniversary of my rape as my affirmation of a positive connection to my body. By that time, I had realized the extent of separation between my body and my mind, and how much the separation had cost me in the way of wholeness. Seeing my physical self through the eyes of the artist gave me a chance to accept myself at a new and deeper level. It created a bridge back to myself that has never since been lost.

~ ~ ~ ~

To summarize, you are a whole human being with a body, a mind, and a spirit. All of you has been hurt, and all of you needs to heal. Furthermore, all of you must work together if any part of you is to fully heal. All you need in order to start are choice and the intention to heal on all levels. This book gives you some ways to begin—or begin again. Other ideas will appear to you as you go through your days. Just know that with time, diligence, attention, and compassion, all of you will be fully you again.

"The journey of knowing fear is in fact the journey of courage."
- Pema Chödrön

Exercises for Chapter 3

The following exercises are designed to help you care for, protect, and strengthen your connection to your body.

Actions you can take

1. **Stop for two or three minutes every day and turn your attention inward.** What sensations do you feel? Do not worry about labeling them as any particular emotions. If you don't like something about your body, that is not a feeling. You do not "feel" ugly, for example. That is an opinion, not a sensation, even if we do use the word "feel" as a synonym for "think" or "evaluate" sometimes. You may feel pressure in your stomach. Your skin may feel dry. You may experience or feel a chill. Those are body feelings. Just identify the physical feelings: aches, itches, tension, nausea, relaxation, fatigue. You do not need to do anything about any of what you feel. The point is simply to notice and to get used to checking in with your body.

2. **Notice how your body feels in different places.** When you enter a store, an office, or a place of worship, or come home, what do you notice? Does your body feel more or less safe in certain places? Do certain people affect how you feel? How about certain kinds of light or darkness, or certain sounds or smells? You might notice a physical

change such as tension or relaxation in various places. You might notice changing emotions such as excitement, nervousness, relief, or something else. If you want, make a note of how you feel or recall it in a journal later. The point is to get in the habit of paying attention to the subtle signals your body gives you all the time in response to your environment.

3. **Make yourself a chart** of daily, weekly, and monthly things you intend to do for your physical well-being. As you do them, check them off. Here is a trick some of my clients have used. Pick up several colors of small stickers and assign an action meaning to each color. For example, blue might stand for meditation, pink for noticing your body sensations, red for exercise, etc. Then, on a big calendar, put a sticker on each day you do those things. You will be able to see at a glance how you are doing at caring for and listening to your body.

4. **Make yourself a master list** in a form you can carry with you, especially if you are just beginning your healing process. On the list, put items such as:

•   Personal phone numbers you may need, such as friends' and family members' numbers

•   Phone numbers for professionals you will want to contact such as doctors, counselors, police, and lawyers

•   Any case numbers and claim numbers

•   A daily or weekly to-do list of tasks

•   A long-term list of things you want to do when you feel better

Then simply carry this list with you until you no longer feel it is serving you.

Questions to ponder

These questions are not meant to be answered quickly. Carry them in your mind for a few days or weeks, and turn them as you contemplate them, considering them from different angles. Your answers may change over time. Simply see where they take you.

1. **Where in your body do you experience peace and well-being?** Do you feel peace in your heart? How about your arms or your legs? Your stomach? Your head? Your eyes? Your face?

2. **How will you know when your body is again at peace?** What part of you will feel different, and how do you expect you will feel? How will you act, or what will you be able to do differently when you are again at peace?

3. **How do you resist caring for your body?** What do you tell yourself about self-care? Which aspects of self-care feel burdensome? Which feel easy? Which do you look forward to doing?

4

Take Care: Your Mind and Your Words

Words have tremendous power. You need your power back, and words can be one of your best allies. Be very careful how you use words. Use your words to help yourself.

What do I mean? First, we are always talking in our heads. We constantly tell ourselves a story about what we are doing, who we are, what we can expect, what is happening around us. This is part of being a human being. If you have ever tried to meditate and have sought to quiet your mind, you know how difficult that can be. When you have been traumatized, you probably talk even more and even faster in your head than you used to. You are bombarding yourself with words every waking moment. It makes sense to be intentionally careful and gentle in the words you use, right?

Self-talk

Beginning immediately, you can either tell yourself a story of strength and hope, or a story of loss, weakness, and grief. You really do have a choice. At the time, I said in my head something like "Oh my God, I will never get through this!" At other times I said things like "I'm doing great! This isn't hurting me anymore. I'm fine." Neither was entirely true, of course, but they seemed true at the time. In fact, there was truth in each story, but none gave a complete picture.

Beginning immediately, you can either tell yourself a story of strength and hope, or a story of loss, weakness, and grief.

In order for the stories you tell yourself to ring true to your deep mind, they must be credible to your heart and to your gut. It does no good to recite affirmations that sound Pollyanna-ish to your ears. When you are in pain, emotional or physical, you just will not believe something like "I know I am on my way to being happy and well." One technique for helping self-talk become credible is to precede positive talk with a phrase like "Even though I don't entirely believe this now…" and follow negative talk with "Even though I feel this way now, I know it will not always be this way."

In order for the stories you tell yourself to ring true to your deep mind, they must be credible to your heart and to your gut.

Changing your self-talk will not necessarily come easily. It did not for me. We are all so accustomed to letting our self-talk run wild and hop all over the place that we do it mostly unconsciously. Here is the key: consciousness. Of course, you will not be able to be conscious of your self-talk every minute. You have a life to lead and things to do, after all. You can, however, train yourself to catch yourself whenever you say anything hurtful to yourself—anything self defeating, anything depressing, or anything unrealistically optimistic. You may need help at first in recognizing these. Chapter 5 speaks more about how to find help.

When you do catch yourself saying something very negative to yourself, take a few seconds to rephrase what you said.

When you do catch yourself saying something very negative to yourself, take a few seconds to rephrase what you said. Add a mental disclaimer and assure yourself that you know you will not always feel such negativity. At the very least, tell yourself and the universe you did not mean what you just said. Then say what is true for you. For example, if you catch yourself telling yourself, "I can't get through all this," stop and immediately say to yourself something like "Even though I feel right now as if I can't get through all this, I know that I can. Cancel. Delete. I am just expressing my pain. I intend to do what I need to do."

You are always listening to your own self-talk.

The idea of watching your words is so important I'll say it again. Be careful and intentional in what you say to yourself. You are always listening to your own self-talk, and part of you will always believe what you say to yourself. Say what will give you strength. You will surely mess up sometimes, but do not worry about that. Just reframe your words when you become aware and go back to your strengths.

Mantras

I encourage you to create a short, easily remembered phrase or mantra for yourself. A mantra consists of words you can say to yourself whenever you need a small lift or even need a verbal lifesaver to hold in a tough time. Mine is simply "You can do this"—whatever "this" means in the moment. A mantra is similar to an affirmation, but I like the word "mantra" better. It conveys a simpler idea. A mantra is a short reminder to yourself of something you know and know that you know. Mantras are not big, elaborate declarations. If you suspect a mantra of not being true, it is not the mantra for you.

If you suspect a mantra of not being true, it is not the mantra for you.

I have used my "You can do this" mantra many times in many difficult situations, but I first used it to get through the aftermath of rape. Sometimes I had to preface it and rephrase it: "Even though I'm tempted not to believe it, I know I can do this." Again, I did not need to specify what "this" was. My mind and heart know what is going on at any particular moment. I did, however, need to *say* the mantra, not just vaguely think about it.

Words are quite literally physical power.

I later saw a vivid demonstration of how self-talk works in a different context altogether. A physical trainer of mine was teaching a class and used me as a volunteer to show the power of words. She had me hold out one arm as she pushed down on it with all her strength. My arm dropped down several inches. Then she had me say, out loud, "I am a weak and unworthy person" ten times. I did not have to believe it. I could even say it with sarcasm. I just had to say the words out loud. She pushed my arm again, and it buckled immediately and dropped all the way to my side. Then she told me to say ten times out loud, "I am a strong and worthy person." Again, it did not matter how I said it except it had to be out loud. She pushed my arm again and it did not budge. I had all the strength I needed to resist her push even though I could feel the pressure she exerted was even more than the other two times. Words are quite literally physical power.

I have experimented with mantras over the years. Mantras do not work if you just imagine them without actually articulating them, at least silently. Out loud is better. In fact, I have learned just about everything has a greater impact if you put it into words. By saying you need to put it in words, I mean actually writing or speaking. It is just too easy to imagine we know or believe what we do not in fact know or believe. Putting something into words means being conscious and deliberate about what you mean. In putting your mantra into words, you clarify exactly what you mean, uncover any resistance you have, recognize where you may be trying to trick yourself, and give yourself a more powerful, positive tool.

Putting something into words means being conscious and deliberate about what you mean.

Journaling

Journaling is another way to use words in support of your healing. What I mean by journaling is that you find someplace to write your truth, fully, clearly, and in all its aspects. Whether your journal is physical such as a journal book or is an electronic file does not matter. What does matter is that you trust it to be secure and private. You need to be able to get access to your journal space readily and privately at some point during every day.

Find someplace to write your truth, fully, clearly, and in all its aspects.

I am not talking about writing "Dear Diary, today I…." Journaling is for putting down your whole truth—how you feel, what you think, what you are worried about, what you feel good about, what wakes you up at night—not just telling what you did. By giving yourself a safe place to write whatever you are going through, with no concern for what anyone else might think, you keep your own healing moving forward.

I imagine it like this. You have a recurring thought you do not like. We all have those. After a while, that thought starts to act like a crosswise log causing a log jam and stopping all your forward flow. The "log" can be something you do not want to acknowledge or something you do not understand.

Here is an example. Maybe you say something to yourself like "I can't stop crying hysterically when I drive near the street where it happened. I have to drive there every day to get to work. I hate this." Maybe you follow it up with something more general that keeps coming up in your self-talk, such as "I'll never feel good again." After a few days (or weeks) of being stuck with this thought, you need to get your thinking moving again. *Write it down.* That is journaling. That will get you unstuck.

When you write in your journal, be honest and complete to the best of your ability. Dig deep into your truth. To illustrate, imagine you wrote the example above about crying and then hating crying when driving past a particular place. Some questions you might ask yourself are these: *Do I imagine it will never change? What do I dislike about the feeling of tears rising in my eyes? To what extent is the whole memory of my attack coming back each time I drive there? What feelings do I have at that location? Fear? Grief? Anger? Despair? What is it about driving to work that makes this drive particularly difficult? What do I assume crying means?* Write it all down until you have exhausted the idea. Then close your journal.

Keep journaling on the same topic on different days until you feel you are finished exploring it. Journaling will not make your feelings of vulnerability, fear, anger, or pain go away. What it will do is keep you moving through them. You may write essentially the same thing for weeks in a row but slowly, and then more rapidly, your experience and your writing will change and evolve. New thoughts will occur to you. You will find it easier to be careful with your self-talk. You will discover more empowering and compassionate things to say to yourself. The more of your truth you can name and write down, the better.

Journaling will not make your feelings of vulnerability, fear, anger, or pain go away. What it will do is keep you moving through them.

Emotions need to be expressed. I believe expression is a physical need. Sometimes, however, you may have no safe place to express the strength and depth of your feelings, especially the negative ones following violence. You cannot always scream or shout or sob or rage, but you can write. It does not have to be eloquent or grammatically correct or even spelled correctly. It just has to be your truth, your emotions, and your reality.

If words do not come to you when you journal, but you have pictures in your imagination, try drawing. Use pencils of differing colors or pastel chalks or watercolor paints. You might even want your journal to be without lines on the pages so you can both write and draw. You can also clip images from magazines and glue them into your journal if they express your experience. Just do not overthink it. Your journal is not an art project. It is a tool for your eyes only to help you advance your healing.

More on the power of words

I was reminded about the power of words when a client of mine was in a deep slump, feeling inadequate, depressed, and unable even to do chores she intended to do. As you have seen, such paralysis can be a consequence of an encounter with violence. My client had been verbally abused by her husband a few days earlier. It was not the first time it had happened. She had cried for a long time and was in considerable emotional pain. His words were a form of violence. When I talked to her, she was calling herself "stupid," "weak," and "whiny." She had adopted some of her husband's abusive words.

After several sessions, she and I did a coaching exercise involving her looking at her situation from various perspectives and experimenting with choosing to think about it in different ways. At first she called herself names and saw herself as pathetic and blameworthy. Eventually, though, she tried considering her husband's explosive behavior as if she were an anthropologist observing the behavior of an alien culture somewhere. From that perspective, she looked back on her experience to see if she could find any signs of inferior intelligence, weakness, or inappropriate whining in herself. She could not. The spell was breaking.

She decided to try out some new, non-judgmental, more neutral words to call herself. She had to struggle for quite some time to find words that felt "true" to her. She decided on "sad," "confused," and "at a disadvantage." She committed to practicing using those words whenever she recalled the incident.

When I talked to her next she was calmer and had new insights into her marriage relationship and her husband's "motivation." She had stopped crying and had begun to feel some hint of strength and resolve in herself. She had major psychological damage that needed healing as well. I referred her to a psychologist, and she began intensive therapy. I later learned she had divorced her husband and gone back to school, not something she could have done had she remained convinced of her "stupidity" or "weakness." Words had the power to begin the transformation of her life.

Here is one last example of how words shape experience. Eight years after I was assaulted, the police caught the rapist. I was asked to go to a lineup to identify him, along with 10 or 12 other women he had also attacked over the years. We women were left in a room together while the lineup was organized and told not to talk to each other. The police simply called us "the victims" and called the room "the victim room." When it was time for the lineup, the captain told the officers to "bring in the victims."

He started the lineup by saying, "Now, Victims, here is how this will work." Afterward, he said, "Victims, please return to the victim room." The police and the prosecutors and defense lawyers talked to each other, occasionally referring to "the victims" as if we were pieces of furniture. At no time were any of us named anything but "victim" until we were called for our individual interviews. Even those were announced to us as the victim interviews.

I felt a hot combination of anger and despair. I wanted to shout at them. At the same time, I felt diminished and the same kind of overwhelming misery I had felt just after I was raped. For that one afternoon, my whole existence had been reduced to no more than my status as a victim. We "victims" had to maintain silence and stand in an unfamiliar, darkened lineup room together, surrounded by police and lawyers who looked at us with pity or did not look at us at all. Each time I heard that word, "victim," my anger and sadness grew.

"Survivor" is a word with deep power. Why not claim that power for yourself?

I knew I was still in one piece, still surviving, after eight years. I was not then and am not now a victim. I banished that word from my vocabulary from then on and adopted "survivor." I survived. So did you. "Survivor" is a word with deep power. Why not claim that power for yourself?

~ ~ ~ ~

"Tears are words waiting to be written."
~ Paulo Coelho

Exercises for Chapter 4

These exercises are designed to help you use your mind and your words effectively to support your own healing.

Actions you can take

1. **Write down all the self-talk you can capture for a day or two.** Write it all down, even when you realize you are saying things to yourself you might not mean, are calling yourself names, or are predicting a terrible future for yourself. The point is to capture what you are saying, not to judge it.

    After each line of self-talk, write down what you truly believe or what you think an objective and wise person would say instead. Begin each with "Even though I do not entirely believe this right now..." if your restatement does not feel quite true to you. As a caring friend, what would you say to reframe that talk?

    Do not feed yourself simplistic platitudes. As with all your use of words to heal, be as truthful as you can be. If sentences feel fake to you, write something that does not feel fake.

    Repeat every few weeks as a check on yourself.

2. **Write a mantra for yourself.** Make yourself a very simple, easily remembered sentence you can recall whenever you feel unsure of your healing. Use it to reassure and remind yourself. By repeating a mantra over time it can influence your whole being. I have included in Appendix A 13 sample mantras that either I have used myself or clients of mine have used. Feel free to use or adapt one of those or write one of your own.

Questions to ponder

1. **If someone you love were feeling as you are now, what would you say to her or him to reframe her or his self-talk?** What words would convey your compassion or caring support?

2. **What thoughts or images give you a feeling of peace?** What words would you use to describe those thoughts or images? What have you heard or read that you found comforting and would like to hear again?

5

Get Help

When life falls apart or is forced off track, as it is when you are a survivor of violence, you can be pushed to your limits. Once you're at your limit, you need someone else to help you find the resources you need to move any further. Furthermore, there is no reason to wait until you hit your limit. Getting help is desirable and even wise at every point of your healing. Here is what can happen if you try to go it alone.

A story

I had a coaching client a few years ago who showed me a vivid example of why survivors *must* connect to other people and get the help they need in the way they need it. She originally started working with me on her goal of changing careers in mid-life. Soon, however, she told me she had a serious health problem: She had diabetes. The last time her blood sugar had been tested in a laboratory, which was several years earlier, it had been dangerously high. Since then, she had not checked her own blood sugar once. She had not seen a doctor and was not intending to do so. She was not thinking about what she was eating. She was not taking any kind of medication.

As we talked further, she told me she was actually afraid to go to a doctor. I assumed she felt some sort of shame about her high blood sugar numbers, but I was wrong. This competent and articulate woman did not want to talk to anyone about any aspect of her body. Something in her allowed her to open the topic to me, however, so I encouraged her to keep talking.

After perhaps four or five more sessions, she revealed that as a teenager she had been gang raped. Four young men had held her down and taken turns raping her. She had been humiliated and traumatized as deeply as I could imagine. She had only told one person in her life before she told me, and the one person she had told at the time was a doctor. Somehow (she did not give me details) that doctor had left her with even more shame and a profound alienation from her body. From then on, she did not want anyone to touch her, ever, in any way. She did not want to feel her feelings. She did not want to know what was happening in her body.

After 40 years had passed, her alienation from her body, and from her experience and truth, was becoming potentially life-threatening. Her refusal to be touched was keeping her from getting vitally needed medical help. The interior pressure cooker in which she had kept her story of rape was about to explode. As she and I worked together, I told her I had survived rape, too. Eventually, she found the courage to visit a new doctor and begin addressing her diabetes. Going to the doctor took all the emotional reserves she could muster, but she did it. I referred her to a mental health professional, and I hope and believe she has found a deeper level of healing now.

Whenever I think of her, I think about the danger of refusing or avoiding help and the risks of acting as though nothing happened.

How do you know when or if you need help?

The simple fact that you have had to survive violence means you could probably benefit from seeking some kind of help. There is nothing wrong with or weak about asking for help—nothing. As in the case of my client who kept it all inside for decades, seeking help is an act of strength and courage. Help may come formally from professionals or informally from friends, family, or groups, or from books.

Seeking help is an act of strength and courage.

If you are unsure about needing or wanting help, here are some clues that you may be ready. You're exhausted and sleep does not help. Even when you have had what seems like adequate physical rest, you still need something more. You do not have any idea what to do. Something feels vaguely broken inside, and it is way beyond what you know how to fix. You are confused or slipping into a numb kind of depression. Despair or hopelessness is setting in. You feel separated from the rest of life. None of your possible futures seems like a future you want. You are anxious much of the time. The things that used to make you happy are no longer enjoyable. These are all signs you would probably do well with help, especially professional help.

Professional help comes in many forms

Therapy and counseling are two obvious kinds of professional help. They are wonderful for giving you a time and place to explore the emotional impact of what happened to you and to gain new insights into why you are reacting the way you are. Your reactions and emotions are likely connected to many other parts of your history and your psyche. A good therapist can help expand your understanding and give you tools to help you cope and grow. Sometimes your health insurance may cover (in whole or in part) the cost of professional help.

Maybe the kind of help you need is spiritual. Chapter 6 discusses spirituality in more detail. Violence and the massive disruption of life that follows it inevitably raise spiritual questions. Some people wonder how their God could let this happen to them. Others blame God for the whole thing. Some doubt the existence of any kind of higher power. Non-believers feel confirmed in their disbelief but do not find comfort in that confirmation. Almost everyone in a violence-related crisis, I think, has to redefine what gives their lives meaning, and what they believe or sense or trust about the spiritual realm.

Spiritual help does not have to be religious, though for some people, formal faith is exactly what is needed. For these people, someone from their tradition can be of tremendous help. Clergy are generally trained to understand the process of spiritual crisis and to link the experience of crisis to the tenets of their particular faith. Spirituality is all about meaning and purpose. Crisis and violence disrupt your entire sense of meaning and how you see yourself fitting in the world. Anyone who can see the bigger picture surrounding your life, who can help you re-formulate your world view, and who can help you strengthen your self-image and connection to your source of meaning is vitally needed during this crisis.

Help can also come from coaches. A crisis is like landing in a strange land without a map, and coaches can help you find or create a map to follow. They are specially trained to do just that. Coaches tend to focus on the future and how you want your future to be, and not as much on how your past was.

In a time of crisis, you do not need someone to tell you what to do, but rather someone who can listen, ask meaningful questions, and point you toward finding your own new way through your world. Therapists, counselors, clergy, and coaches can do that for you.

So why do people not ask for help?

One big reason people do not get help is fear—fear of being seen as weak, fear of what they will learn that they would rather not know, fear that help will just give them more to worry about or more to have to do. Some people are reluctant to go into therapy in particular because they do not know what therapy feels like or how it works. They are afraid it will make them feel worse. The truth is, it might feel worse in some ways for a while as the pieces inside you rearrange themselves into a bigger whole. In the long run, however, good help from a trained therapist will always make matters easier.

> ### Good help from a trained therapist will always make matters easier.

Another big and related reason people do not ask for help is they have a self-image of independence. Self-image is especially tough for smart, capable, accomplished people. They know they can handle just about anything and know they have overcome major obstacles before. They got their education, found their partners, had their kids, learned to drive or swim or ride a bike. They have met professional and personal challenges, earned promotions, achieved recognition. They have a deep inner self-image of a doer, and see themselves as strong and effective people. Yet here they are, in a crisis that has stopped them cold. Their instinct is to go at it harder, do more, sleep less, push the crisis aside, pretend everything is as it was. The problem is that doing more soon becomes a losing strategy.

Everything is not as it was and never will be again. The violence that happened will not be pushed aside. If your emotions are forced underground, they will eventually erupt in some particularly ugly or disturbing form. Despite my general ability to handle challenges before I was raped, afterward I was horrified to find myself not functioning well at all. I felt as if there was not much left inside me for coping with ordinary life. I felt I was less valuable as a person and an employee because of my new limitations. Now I recognize those feelings as partly natural and partly a combination of depression and spiritual crisis. Seek help before your sense of self-worth becomes damaged and you feel diminished and inadequate.

Seek help before your sense of self-worth becomes damaged.

Embarrassment stops some people from getting help. If they experience profound humiliation during the violent attack, as many survivors do, they may not want to re-open those feelings by talking about what happened. Many people live in a culture that views getting psychological or even spiritual help as self-indulgent or weak. In these cases, even when survivors recognize they do need help, cultural norms make them feel embarrassed by their own need.

No matter what happened to you, you know you might be judged as weak or flawed if you cannot—or choose not to—go it alone. We all have powerful "strong loner" cultural ideals. Think about the characters Katniss Everdeen in *The Hunger Games,* Ellen Ripley in *Alien,* and nearly every movie role played by John Wayne, Clint Eastwood, or Bruce Willis.

Admitting the need for help means you have to challenge the cultural ideals you have been assimilating for a long time.

Society still stigmatizes mental health services in particular, and this stigma stops many people. The stigma works especially against men. *MaleSurvivor*, a non-profit organization serving men who have faced sexual assault, estimates that the average time between a man being victimized by rape and his talking about it *at all* is twenty years! I can barely imagine the solitary pain of carrying both the experience of violence and shame or humiliation for more than two decades.

Stigma works especially against men.

Then there is the fear of the experience itself of being helped. Whether the help is therapy, counseling, or spiritual direction—and I have been a client of all—you may not know how it works. Will it go on forever? Will you have to talk about your childhood? Will you be judged? Will you be diagnosed? What will it cost? Where will you find the time? How much will it help? What if you do not know what is wrong and cannot think of what to say? Hundreds of such questions arise the minute you contemplate asking for professional help. My recommendation for you is this: Do it anyway and find out.

Some fear they will trust the wrong person. They worry they will go for help and instead be judged or shamed, misunderstood or ignored. They fear the help will not actually help, and their despair and isolation could deepen and cause more suffering than they already have.

Whenever you seek help and whatever help you find, you always have a right to quit and go somewhere else. If you do not feel strengthened after spending a little time with a helping professional, do not go back. Even if you see someone for several sessions, if you do not think the help you are getting is effective, you can stop. Keep looking. I changed therapists and counselors seven times over the years, and that does not even count the two or three spiritual teachers I also worked with. It was not that any were inadequate. I got something important I needed from each—one piece of my puzzle—and then I moved on each time I needed something more. You can do the same.

If you do not think the help you are getting is effective, you can stop.

How to find and use professional help

Ask for referrals if you do not know who you want to go to for help. Ask friends, and even acquaintances if you trust their judgment. Sometimes there may be online directories you can consult. Ask people who may know: your doctor, another type of healer such as a chiropractor, or your clergy. Ask for a local referral from a crisis phone line. Use your imagination. For example, maybe you see an accountant who holds many of your same values. She or he may know of a counselor with similar values. If you work for an employer that offers its employees assistance in locating community resources, use the service.

Remind yourself it takes real strength to ask for help. The fact you are asking is proof of your strength, not your weakness. Pretending to be strong when you do not feel strong is usually foolish. It is also usually destructive. Pull out your strength mantra, and dial the phone or send the appointment request.

> ## The fact you are asking for help is proof of your strength, not your weakness.

If worry about the stigma society places on mental health services is stopping you, get help from a clergy member or a coach. Coaching started out with business executives so the stigma does not usually attach to coaching. Spiritual help and direction offer wisdom and support that may make it feel more comfortable for you than anything feeling more "medical." Seeing these professionals will not make you or anyone else think of you as "sick."

Remember again: You have control in any professional help situation. You set the speed. You decide how long it goes on and how long it is useful to you. You always have a choice about what you say and how much of yourself you reveal.

> ## You always have a choice about what you say and how much of yourself you reveal.

Schedule an exploratory session so you can size up the person. See how you feel when you talk with him or her. Notice if your stomach goes into a knot or if you feel relief and comfort. Your work in tuning in to your body, as described in Chapter 1, will help you in assessing potential helpers. You can say *no* if someone feels wrong to you. You do not need to know why she or he feels wrong; you can simply rely on your intuition. Just be aware there is a difference between resistance in you coming from your fears and characteristics in the counselor, meaning he or she simply is not a fit for you. If you feel uncomfortable, ask yourself if the problem is you or the counselor. Your heart and your gut will give you your answer.

Getting help from friends

Immediately after a violent attack, the crisis itself gives you plenty to do. You may, however, need practical help with the rest of life. You may need someone else to clean your kitchen floors when you need your time to write in your journal or make calls, or you are just feeling too "down" to get up and do it. You may need someone to help get groceries or prepare your food. Friends can do these things.

Help from friends is necessarily limited, however. Friendship is a reciprocal relationship. In a friendship, you both give and receive, and each have your own ups and downs. In the crisis following an attack you may not be able to give much back for a long time. When one of my friends became exhausted with me, got angry, and told me I could not expect so much of her, she was probably right. I had huge needs and she had a regular life to lead. The crisis lasted much, much longer for me than it did for her. It will always last longer for you than for your friends.

In the crisis following an attack you may not be able to give much back for a long time.

Because there are built-in limits to what friends and even spouses and partners can do, I encourage you to consider professional help for a while if at all possible.

Groups

Many different types of support groups exist. Some groups are organized specifically for survivors of trauma. Your doctor, a local hospital, or your place of worship may know of survivor groups in your area. Other groups, such as the various 12-step addiction-recovery groups based on the Alcoholics Anonymous model, provide peer support for stopping addictive or compulsive behaviors. The Depression and Bipolar Support Alliance (DBSA) offers peer support groups in many areas and online for people suffering from depression or bipolar disorder and for their family members. See Appendix B for contact information for some groups.

The advantage of a group is the chance to talk with others who "get" it without you having to explain yourself. A disadvantage is sometimes a group is ineffective, especially a peer-led group, if one person dominates it or is disrespectful. Nonetheless, the support of a group can be powerful.

Help from the written word

Help can be had from books. If I did not believe that, I would not have written this one. Many, many books exist able to give you insight into healing, into trauma, into spirituality, into psychology, into violence itself. Search for terms like "healing" or "survivor." There are also countless magazine articles, websites, and, increasingly, blogs.

Apply the same standards you would apply to seeking help in person. If the information you are reading does not resonate with you, let it go. If you do not feel the writer is relating to situations like yours, stop reading. If, however, you find strength, hope, or understanding, keep reading. By hearing or reading of someone else's experience, you can feel less isolated with your own. You may also see how you are different and in the process gain insight into your own unique healing path.

About PTSD

Some survivors of violence suffer from post-traumatic stress disorder, or PTSD. Therefore, I want to describe it briefly along with some of its treatments.

The term "post-traumatic stress disorder" did not exist before the mid-1970s when it began to be used to describe the psychological effects of combat on Vietnam War veterans. The symptoms and the phenomenon no doubt existed long before the term was coined. At earlier times among war veterans, the symptoms were called "shell shock" and "battle fatigue." Those who suffered from it were sometimes called "malingerers" or "cowards." Among civilians, the general term "anxiety" was often used to refer to PTSD symptoms.

In simple terms, PTSD arises from experiences of exceptionally threatening events where survivors felt afraid for their lives or physical well-being and where they faced extreme fear, helplessness, or horror. They continue to have intense and intrusive "flashback" experiences that are deeply disturbing. They experience ongoing anxiety or find they are avoiding places, activities, or even thoughts that remind them of their original trauma. A pattern of avoidance begins to interfere with normal life. Many who survive violence, even extreme violence, will not develop PTSD, but those who do have a particularly painful time.

Many who survive violence, even extreme violence, will not develop PTSD, but those who do have a particularly painful time.

I did develop PTSD. I had a few moments of intense anxiety that seemed to come out of nowhere but that make sense in retrospect. One such episode came when I went back to graduate school about two and a half years after my rape. I entered a program with a large majority of men in it. When I walked in on the first day to register and buy my books, I started shaking uncontrollably. I was nearly in tears after only half an hour. Before then and after my rape, I had spent my time around mostly women. The presence of dozens of men—most younger, all energetic, some downright aggressive—terrified me. I felt unable even to stay in the building, let alone do the work of graduate school.

I panicked. I walked straight to Student Health Services, into their mental health department and said "I need to see somebody as soon as possible." The next day, I saw a psychologist there and began the life-saving journey that would go on for the next 30 years.

Another episode came when I had dental work done, about six years after my rape. The hygienist put on latex gloves and put her finger in my mouth such that the glove was beneath my nose. I could smell the latex. I had a classic PTSD flashback. It was not that my mind thought I was really back in the room with the rapist, but my body thought it was. I understood then how my body's cells have all my memory within them. My body remembered the smell of latex, and that memory surfaced abruptly as I bit the hygienist's finger without thinking. I pushed her hand away from my face and cried. Images raced through my mind of knives and blood, and I felt a familiar sickening tension in the floor of my pelvis. I had to leave.

PTSD is currently considered to be a significant mental health problem. It is generally treated with talk therapy and appropriate medications. Other therapeutic techniques, such as Eye Movement Desensitization and Reprocessing (EMDR), are also effective at relieving the symptoms of PTSD. Other therapists and doctors recommend a technique called Emotional Freedom Technique (EFT). You can easily find more information about either EMDR or EFT online or in the library.

I was fortunate eventually to find a therapist skilled at using the EMDR technique. When I had a third flashback experience on a date with a slightly too-aggressive man, she was there for me. Even though I did not recognize the connection to my rape, she did recognize it and recommended EMDR. After several sessions my anxiety reactions truly cleared at a deep level, and they have not returned since.

If you think you may be suffering from PTSD and those symptoms are interfering in your life, I strongly urge you to consult a mental health professional.

Choosing which kind of help to seek when

Following is a brief guide to help you identify where you want to start looking for help.

• **Therapists and counselors** provide psychological help. Some are familiar with and even specialize in treating PTSD. Different therapists have different philosophies and methods, and may be oriented toward working with you for a long time in depth or toward working with you for a relatively shorter period. The cost of some professional mental health services may be covered by health insurance. If you are experiencing suicidal thoughts or are afraid you are breaking down somehow, mental health professionals are definitely the help to seek.

• **Doctors and other health professionals** are critically important if you have physical injuries. Your doctor may also be a resource for finding other kinds of help. Psychiatrists can prescribe medications to help you manage severe and distressing symptoms. Alternative healers, such as naturopaths, homeopaths, body workers, or energy workers, provide help for your body as you deal with the aftermath of violence.

• **Clergy** provide spiritual guidance, support, and help in understanding your crisis from the perspective of your religion. Some clergy work with clients from religions other than their own or who do not profess any religion. If you are experiencing a loss of meaning or purpose in your life or alienation from God as you understand God, you are having a spiritual crisis. Consider seeking out a clergy member for help.

• **Life coaches** emphasize the future and help you envision what you want, set goals, formulate plans, and find ways to keep your motivation to reach your goals energized and focused. A coach who has experience with surviving violence may be able to help you earlier in your healing than other coaches. You can work with a coach at the same time as you work with a mental health professional or a clergy member.

• **Groups** are particularly helpful when you need to tell your story to people who can understand because they have been there, too. Groups are also valuable if you are someone who generally feels energized and supported by being around people. When you need advice or want the perspective of someone else who gone through healing before you, members of a group may be the perfect people to ask. Generally, when you join a group you will need to make some minimum commitment to continue participating and to being supportive to other members.

• **Friends, family, and partners** may be able to provide wonderful help, and they may not be. Different members of your family may be able to help in different ways. For example, some may not be able to hear what you have been through because your story frightens them, but they can give you practical assistance. Others may be able to listen to you as you process your story many times. Some may have special skills to offer such as cooking or yard care. Some may be able to accompany you to your medical or legal appointments. When you ask for help from family or friends, stay alert to signs they are not giving you what you need. Find a graceful way to step back if you feel you are being judged or blamed, or you feel they are taking over what you need to do for yourself.

• **Neighbors** can help you in a number of ways, but unless you consider a neighbor to be a close friend, recognize the help may be limited to non-emotional help. Neighbors can help in such areas as giving you transportation periodically, caring for your home should you need to be away for a while, or running errands when you feel overwhelmed.

• **Books, websites, and blogs** can help you feel less alone and give you other perspectives on the challenges facing you. These have the advantage of being available to you at any time and when you are alone. At times, you may need both help and privacy for a while, and written materials can be there for you then.

~~~~

My main message to you about help is: Get it. I truly believe the more you can open yourself to receiving help from many sources, in person or in print, the more completely you can heal.

"If you bring forth what is within you, what you bring forth will save you.
If you do not bring forth what is within you, what you do not bring forth
will destroy you."
~ The Gnostic Gospel of Thomas

Exercises for Chapter 5

These exercises are designed to support you in deciding if and when you need help, and in getting the help you need.

Actions you can take

1. **Identify and list the contact information for several help resources in your area.** You need not necessarily contact them. Just have the list ready if there comes a time you want to contact someone. Who might give you a referral or recommendation? What resources can you find online?

2. **Use your journal to explore any resistance you may have to getting help.** List the pros and the cons *for you* of seeking professional help. Consider such questions as: What do you expect help to feel like? How much do you think your friends or family are able or willing to do for you? What images come to you when you think about getting help? What fears arise in you around the idea of help?

Questions to ponder

1. **What are your toughest challenges both now and for the next year or so?** Do you need practical help with the tasks of life? Is fear, anger,

or grief starting to overwhelm you? Are you finding your spiritual beliefs and values shaken? What calls to you most right now?

2. **What is your highest hope if you were to get professional help?** How do you imagine you would feel if therapy, counseling, or spiritual direction were highly effective for you? What do you stand to gain?

6

Take Care: Your Spirit

Spiritual healing, I believe, is a critically important part of healing from violence. You do not need to be religious or hold any particular religious beliefs in order to need healing of your spirit.

You do not need to be religious or hold any particular religious beliefs in order to need healing of your spirit.

I was baffled during my healing years by the contradiction between how hard I had fought to stay alive and how easily I later came to the point of wanting to end my own life. I understood later I was experiencing a severe spiritual crisis. I learned such a crisis is predictable and is a frequent consequence of having faced violence. In order to heal fully, I absolutely had to face this spiritual crisis and find a firm spiritual foundation on which to stand. I am convinced that all survivors of violence need to attend to their spiritual needs as well as other needs.

Spirit collapse: my experience

I had to work to keep myself alive through the night I was attacked and again after. During my rape experience, a part of my being was focused simply on how to get out alive. That part of me focused on where within the darkness the knife was, where the rapist was, where the door was, where my keys and my car were. Twelve years later, I faced a health crisis when I was diagnosed with cervical cancer. At that time, I had to work in a different way to stay alive. I had to submit to frightening medical treatments and procedures, including two that were deeply terrifying to me, given my history of having had my body forcibly invaded.

My work to stay alive was practical and psychological at first. I had to push through fears, summon courage, find ways to care for my body and ways to manage the constant anxiety inside. I struggled with the simplest self-care—food and sleep—but I did get through it. When I had to have cancer surgery, I taught myself new relaxation techniques and used them. I used music. I used hypnosis. I tried everything I could think of or any of my friends suggested. And I succeeded. I was alive.

Then in the 13th year after my rape, and again in the 18th year, and yet again in the 28th year, I found myself thinking I wanted to be dead. I wanted to give up. I wanted to go out to the garage with the door closed, turn on my car engine, and go to sleep for good. I knew I had worked hard to keep and heal my life, and now I seemed to want to throw it away. I was also conscious of how tired I was and how much I craved rest. I was exhausted by the feeling of being unsupported in the world and the fear that I would never really heal.

The first time my spirit collapsed, it was in response to someone's refusal to help me when I lost a job. The person who said *no* to me was a professional colleague who was suffering from untreatable depression. I now see he was desperately trying to shore up his own seriously weakened sense of self. The blow to my ego, however, exposed the fragility of my mental health.

I got as far as the car in the garage with my keys in the ignition when I remembered my cat inside my house. My heart hurt at the thought of her being left alone, and I cried. That seemed to open a line to a voice inside me that I have since learned to trust—the voice of my own higher self or of a benevolent Other (I see no need to distinguish the two). The voice asked, "Are you willing to die for this man's sickness?" My ordinary consciousness could never have posed such a question. It was the exact right question to break through my darkness. Of course I was not willing to die for his sickness. Sobbing, I went back inside, picked up my cat, and held her, crying into her fur until I was able to fall asleep.

No amount of professional or public success can fill the emptiness created by spiritual damage.

The second time there was no obvious event triggering my despair, but again my job and professional status were in jeopardy. Until then I had used my professional accomplishments to bolster the spiritually weakened parts of myself. Now I realize no amount of professional or public success can fill the emptiness created by spiritual damage. That lesson was yet to come, however.

The second time I contemplated suicide, I took my same cat out to the car in the garage with me. I decided to take her into death with me so I would not be stopped by my concern for her. She went to the car willingly (a surprise!) and sat quietly beside me in the car in the locked garage while I put the key into the ignition. That time there were no voices in my mind. Nothing came to stop me. I sat for more than an hour holding the key, my mind racing through my memories. My pain engulfed me and suddenly I had the thought that I did not actually want to be dead; I just wanted my life not to hurt so horribly. I just did not want to feel so desperately alone. The realization was enough. I took the key out of ignition and went inside, slumped into my big chair, and sat staring and crying for most of the night.

The third time came yet again in the aftermath of a professional setback. I was not that good at fighting for money or status, so I tended to lose those kinds of fights. By that time, I had been seeing a therapist for several years. I had also found the beginnings of new spiritual ground, which I will describe shortly. As I started sliding into darkness yet again, I had enough self-awareness to put notes around my house, including one on the door to my attached garage, saying "Suicide is not an option."

I remembered how hurt and angry I had been when a close friend actually had committed suicide years earlier. I was furious she would just walk out on all of us who cared about her. I said if she were to come back to life, I would be tempted to kill her all over again. I swore I would never make anyone else feel that way about me. That was a promise I forgot for a while but remembered as I put up my notes.

The night I felt completely overwhelmed—again—by self-doubt, spiritual fatigue, emptiness, meaninglessness, and hopelessness, I picked up my keys and headed toward the garage when I saw one of my notes. I fell to the floor right there in my entryway, covered my eyes with my hands, and cried out loud from somewhere in the core of me, "If suicide is not an option, then somebody has got to help me!" It was a moment of total surrender; my ego-self gave up for good trying to save me.

I said those words and instantly everything—and I do mean everything—inside me shifted. I no longer wanted to die at all. The feeling has never returned in the decade and a half since that night. Nor do I have any fear it will ever return. My emotions have fluctuated up and down since then, to be sure, but never once have I felt such desperate emptiness. Somebody did help me, somebody or something not of my ordinary consciousness. After that night, I can be certain I am not alone in the universe. That knowledge has made all the difference.

Call it God, call it Spirit Guide, call it Higher Self or Higher Power, call it by any name; the name does not matter. The name is not the same as what actually is. The knowing is what matters. The help that came to me that night finally filled the spiritual emptiness consuming my life that was magnified by my violent rape. Because of that night, I truly believe full healing from violence requires healing your spirit as well as your body and mind.

My process of healing did not magically end right then. I do not think there is any end to healing, and that is okay. My process was transformed, however. I may have continued to feel pain from time to time, but I no longer suffered in despair in addition to the pain. I no longer felt empty. I have no longer wanted to give up on life.

I have made a number of radical life changes since that day. I changed careers; I moved to a new and very different city; and I got married for the first time. Despite how positive these changes were, they all entailed losses as well and forced me to say goodbye to familiar parts of my world. The skills I developed in caring for myself after my rape, physically, emotionally, and spiritually, have helped me immeasurably through all these losses and transitions.

Let me move on to the question of how you find healing for your spirit.

A few words on the role of religion

Religion is of paramount importance to many, many people. Tomes have been written about why we humans turn to religion. Within every religious doctrine, there are at least partial answers to some of our deepest questions: *Who am I? Why am I here? What is the meaning of my life? How do I live a "good" life? What am I supposed to do? What happens when my life ends? What is real? Is there more than what I see? What is Divinity?*

Furthermore, religious experience is not intellectual experience. Belief cannot be forced or coerced; belief either is or is not. When we do believe a doctrine, supported by the structures of our religion, our beliefs are vital to our individual lives, our families' lives, and our communities' lives.

Formal religious institutions (churches, temples, synagogues, mosques) have played critical positive roles in society, from binding communities together, caring directly for those who are disadvantaged, reinforcing deep moral values, giving comfort to those bereaved, recognizing and celebrating the passages of life, providing a means for individuals to worship and experience awe, and creating opportunities for service to each other. And, of course, history is also full of horrible religious wars because often the anchoring beliefs in one religion have called for extinguishing other beliefs and killing the people who hold them.

I was brought up in Protestant Christianity. If you had asked me early enough in my life if I believed in Christian orthodoxy, I would have answered *yes*. I still acknowledge the truth of much of what I was taught, but for me, the beliefs were just not real enough when I faced a knife in the middle of the night.

I had always had a fairly deep sense of there being a God, but that sense was severely shaken by the trauma of violence. After many years of suffering, a deeper part of me finally opened to knowledge and certainty that, for me, transcends belief.

If you have experienced trauma and you find your religion truly nurtures your soul, strengthens you, and supports you, then you are genuinely blessed. Embrace your religion fully. Become active, attend worship times, serve within your religious community. Let its tenets fill you and awaken the deepest parts of your spirit. Adopt a religious practice, daily if you can. You need all of you awakened in order to heal fully from violence. Formal religion, especially if you have known it from childhood, can open that consciousness for you. Your religion can be your path to spiritual healing.

If, however, you are more like me and find something strangely missing in what you have been taught, no matter how much you wish it were otherwise, keep going. Keep searching until you find what fills you. I believe you will find it. I think you will find it within yourself in a place that something or somebody in the world will help you awaken. Following are some suggestions on how to go about your spiritual search.

Meditation

> *"Be still and know that I am God."*
> ~ *Psalms 46:10*

Though I am not big on quoting sacred texts from any religion, I have long loved this one biblical passage. Being still is at the heart of meditation and prayer. Nothing could be further from our ordinary way of living or from the inner chaos after you have survived an encounter with violence. When I speak of meditation, I am referring to a regular practice of taking time out to be quiet. It may involve contemplating the spiritual domain or it may not. It may involve focusing on a repetitive mantra or your breath, or it may not. It may involve intentional, mindful movement, or it may involve physical stillness.

There are many forms of meditation, and many books written about them and recordings made to induce them. You will have no trouble finding dozens of resources (teachers, DVDs, CDs, books, mediation centers) if you want them. I want to give you some of my perspective on this widespread and ancient practice.

Let me say right up-front I am not a long-term meditator, though I have often wished I were. I do, however, keep coming back to the practice as my spirituality evolves and my life changes. As I write now, I am again meditating most every day, but I completely understand the resistance and difficulty you might feel. What I have to say is therefore from the perspective of a beginner, not an expert, certainly not a master. Even if you resist the idea of meditation, I urge you to try it anyway. There are significant benefits for a survivor of violence.

Even if you resist the idea of meditation, I urge you to try it anyway. There are significant benefits for a survivor of violence.

First, let me refute some stereotypes and myths about meditation. One myth says meditation involves emptying your mind. Not likely. Our minds race all the time and generate thoughts almost constantly. We tell ourselves stories and assess the world nearly every minute we are awake. It seems to me obvious that we are not likely to be able simply to turn all that thinking off, no matter how many hours or years we practice. We will always be human, and constant storytelling is, I believe, part of being human. That is why I urged you to pay attention to the words you are telling yourself and choose those that empower you. Even if you cannot completely dismiss the thoughts of violence for even a minute, meditation is still worthwhile. Meditating will still bring you some measure of relief.

Meditation does not mean the absence of thought but rather makes us aware the part of us behind and beyond the thoughts. Some have called this the "observer self." I think of it as the quiet spot in the center of me while I stand in a swirling world of my memories, stories, fears, dreams, and imaginings. I picture ripples in a body of water or sound waves traveling from a silent, quiet, motionless point. When I meditate, I do my best to open my awareness to that quiet part of me and let the thoughts and stories come and go, ripple away from me without following them, without engaging with them, without resisting them or reacting to them in any way.

Drifting away does not mean meditation is not worth doing or not "working."

And, of course, I fail repeatedly each time I sit for meditation. Drifting away does not mean meditation is not worth doing or not "working." When I become aware I have again wandered off center into some past or future story, I intentionally and as gently as I can, bring myself back to my quiet center to rest there for as long as I can before another story seduces me away again. Over and over. Drift, return, drift, return. I now know that is okay.

Another myth about meditation says if you do not do it exactly as one teacher or another has taught, it may have no value at all. I just do not believe that. I believe the mere act of taking time out regularly, every day if possible, to be quiet and to slow the onslaught of your mind's activity, has benefit. Even with "failures" throughout a meditation session, there is still power and value in the practice. Researchers from several fields have studied meditators in recent years. They seem to be coming to similar conclusions: that there are physical and emotional benefits to meditation. Meditation does seem to be a "just do it" kind of thing. Just do it and do not worry about it. If you do, it will "work."

Meditation does not always mean physical stillness. If you prefer, you can adopt a more physically active meditative practice to bring you into mindful presence. Examples are yoga, tai chi, qigong, art, dance, music, even martial art. Mindful, intentional slow walking is also a meditative practice.

Your goal in meditation is to be fully focused in present time, neither ruminating over the past nor anticipating or fearing the future. The present is the only time when you can heal. The present can seem infinitesimally small compared to the enormity of time stretching out before and after it, but the present is the only place you ever are. You only truly exist, always, in the present.

The present can seem infinitesimally small compared to the enormity of time stretching out before and after it, but the present is the only place you ever are.

Peace and the connection to your deep soul reside in the present, the now, the still point. What happened to you in your past, awful though it might have been, is no longer here now that you have survived. It is only memory. To meditate and seek to rest in present time is to let the memory go for a while, to take a break, to give yourself a small gift of peace, to be both quiet and fully alive. The healing power of such moments is immense, more than you might imagine.

Prayer

Praying is what you are doing when your intention is to communicate directly with the Divine, however you conceive the Divine to be. All forms of prayer can contribute to your healing at this spirit level, but one form stands out.

Prayer is more active than meditation when your prayer is a prayer of supplication (asking for something) or thanksgiving. In those cases, you may be the one doing the talking to the Divine. Likewise, prayers of adoration and praise, as we see in the writings and music of many traditions, may involve words from you. There are also prayers of confession when you seek to clear your spirit of guilt or shame. When you are praying these kinds of prayer, you may not be listening at those moments. I have come to believe the listening kind of prayer is most important for healing.

Contemplative prayer is a form very close to other forms of meditation. Contemplative prayer, like all meditation, also calls for inner quiet and openness. You do not talk in contemplative prayer; you listen. Some contemplative prayers may be focused on passages from sacred texts; some may be focused on a sacred word or an object (an icon, candle flame, or image). Some may be simple quiet and moments of waiting, resting in the present and allowing Divine presence to be sensed or known. Having been raised Christian, I found the contemplative prayer form of Centering Prayer to be especially helpful.

Every spiritual tradition offers one or more forms of contemplative prayer. If you feel called to connect to the Divine consciously, I urge you to learn and embrace one of those forms.

Patience and acceptance

Patience can be a tough goal, especially if you are someone like me who handles life by doing something and who dislikes standing still. Healing after violence, however, as you now know, takes a lot of time. Everything in you may want to rush your process and get back to some sort of "normal" as fast as possible, but you simply cannot. Your body, mind, and spirit all need time. Healing is an ongoing process, not a goal.

If you stay focused on how much you *do not* feel like you, it will take longer to feel as if you *are* truly you again.

Here is a truth you may not like: If you stay focused on how much you *do not* feel like you, it will take longer to feel as if you *are* truly you again. You may not be able at all to get back to feeling fully you. You will certainly cause yourself suffering. If you have some picture in your mind of how you "should" be and feel, then see your life does not match that idealized picture, the resulting disappointment, even despair, is indeed painful. The pain will slow your healing, just as physical pain slows the healing of physical wounds.

I blew it on this one in a big way. I pushed myself to get back to work, to go back to dating, to doing all sorts of things—from dancing to reading to hiking to going to graduate school—all within just the first two years. All that busy-ness may have made me feel better and more competent for a few minutes or days. However, as my previous story shows, after more than a decade, something deeper demanded my attention.

> Acceptance has nothing to do with making
> anything okay. It has only to do with acknowledging
> what actually is.

Acceptance is another central part of spiritual healing. But how, you may ask, can you accept violence when it seems to be completely unacceptable? This knot was untangled for me by a spiritual teacher who defined acceptance simply as seeing with the mind and knowing with the heart. Nothing more. Not liking, not condoning, not even tolerating. Just seeing and knowing. Acceptance now for me means looking at reality squarely and knowing, both in my mind and my heart, what is actually true. Acceptance has nothing to do with making anything okay. It has only to do with acknowledging what actually is.

In that light, nothing is truly unacceptable. You can detest something and still accept it as part of reality. Again, acceptance is simply allowing yourself to see the full truth of what actually is, what happened, how you now are—without judgment, without trying to rush to some different future, and without denying some part of your past. We are accustomed to judging and rejecting the parts of life we do not like, so shifting to acceptance may be counterintuitive and difficult at first. The practice of bringing your awareness to the present moment, as you do in meditation, will help you find acceptance, will give you greater patience, and so will help you heal.

Service

Doing something—almost anything—for the benefit of someone else will give you back more of yourself. Service directly reminds you how all people are interconnected. It is a powerful tool in your search for spiritual growth and healing. When you witness and meet the needs of someone else, for a moment you are not aware of your own. You are more aware of how their need is like your needs and how you are alike as fellow humans. You are bigger, and you see more than your own struggle.

Service directly reminds you how all people are interconnected.

A key principle in Alcoholics Anonymous and all other 12-step recovery programs is that people in recovery from an addiction can best help themselves by helping others. In fact, the 12th step reads: "Having had a spiritual awakening as the result of these Steps, we tried to carry this message to [others who suffer,] and to practice these principles in all our affairs." It is precisely the community of people who see themselves in each other that is able to support the healing and recovery of each one. No one person is better than another, no one is the teacher and no one is the student. Equals helping equals means successful healing.

Look for opportunities where your abilities match someone else's needs.

Any kind of service can support your own healing. Look for opportunities where your abilities match someone else's needs. Service could be anything from ladling soup at a soup kitchen to mentoring a child to visiting someone near the end of life to helping a community group plant trees or stuffing envelopes for a non-profit group's mailing.

Here are a few more specific examples. One of my clients was a massage therapist. She volunteered to give free massages to people newly diagnosed with life-threatening illnesses. A man I know who is a magician taught magic to kids at risk of being pulled into gangs in order to give them a sense of mastery without violence. Another woman, a teacher with free time during the summers, committed to going on mission trips each year with her church to help build schools and clinics in other countries.

The opportunities to give service are almost limitless. Sadly, the unmet needs within most of our communities are enormous. Many cities and towns have directories of volunteer opportunities or at least of service organizations who are seeking volunteers. Houses of worship in nearly any religion are likely to have volunteer opportunities, either within their own walls or as their mission in the world.

Giving service can also be a momentary act of kindness that helps another. You see someone with a cane struggling to get through a doorway so you hold the door open. You smile respectfully at a homeless person on the street. Your smile may be more valuable than money. A client of mine, while driving, saw a child lose his ball on a sloping sidewalk and saw the ball bounce rapidly downhill. The child could not have caught it before it rolled into a busy street. She turned her car around, retrieved the ball, and returned it to the child. She reported her entire day was brightened by the child's smile.

Here are some things I did as service to give you a few more examples. I served hot meals to homeless people, sang with a chorus in nursing homes and on children's hospital wards, and painted houses in lower-income neighborhoods, even though I am not a good singer or painter, and make a mess when I serve soup. I also did public speaking, survivor advocacy, and community education for a rape crisis center. I worked actively to support legislative changes to ease the way for future survivors of violence and help them maintain their dignity and privacy. With each of these acts I know I felt stronger and more like the person I had been before violence came into my life.

The idea is to reach outside yourself. As you step out of yourself more, you will inevitably be "in" yourself more as well.

Gratitude

"What is there to be grateful for?" I can almost hear my own voice from a few years ago. The idea of expressing gratitude seemed to me, and may seem to you, to be a mental exercise, a gimmick, a way of denying the pain of actual experience. What is there to be grateful for? Everything. Of course, I am not glad there is violence in the world, but I can be grateful for the way the dark experiences in life can open pathways to wholeness that might otherwise never be found.

Gratitude is a shift in focus, a way of paying attention to certain aspects of life right in front of you.

Gratitude is a shift in focus, a way of paying attention to certain aspects of life right in front of you. Think about the famous black and white optical illusion that, when you focus on the black, appears to be the outline of a goblet but, when you focus on the white, reveals two silhouetted people facing each other. Both images are there at all times. You can choose which one you see.

Similarly, even in the crisis and chaos of emotions following a violent attack, you still can shift your focus. You can appreciate the friends or professionals who come into your life and help you. You can see the beauty in sunshine or flowers. In giving thanks, you may feel Divine presence. You can certainly recognize the simple fact you have survived and be grateful for life and for the strength you needed and still have that allowed you to survive.

When I finally did go to the police three days after I was raped, I told the detective I felt bad about leaving my window open that night. He immediately said I had had every right to have my window open; the rapist had no right to climb through it. I was immensely grateful for that detective at the time and have been increasingly grateful for him ever since. Sadly, not every survivor gets such reassurance from the police, I realize. I was helped at a terrible time in an important way. By later focusing on my gratitude for that help, I also kept moving forward in my healing.

During my own periods of depression, I adopted the practice of writing down three things at the end of each day for which I felt gratitude. I allowed myself to repeat the same things from day to day. Some days I had moments of wonder, an exceptional sunset, or a surprise note of encouragement from a friend. Some days, all I could come up with were extremely simple ideas like "I am grateful I can breathe" and "I am grateful I can move my arms." It did not matter how small or how profound. The shift to gratitude each day undoubtedly helped me lift my own spirit.

I recently heard a doctor describe how he advises a similar daily practice for his patients. He asks them to name five people at the end of each day for whom they are grateful and to write down why they have chosen each person. Again, shifting focus to gratitude helps the patients heal in much the same way medicine and surgery do.

Gratitude increases both your emotional and your spiritual strength. When your focus is on the things around you that nourish you, enrich you, or calm you, and the people who help you, support you, or encourage you, you automatically increase the positive side of yourself.

As you choose to heal, why would you not choose to practice gratitude to help yourself?

An obstacle: anger at God

I underestimated the extent to which rape would damage my connection to God. Being raped made me deeply and profoundly angry. Part of me blamed God for letting it happen. Many of my clients have said similar things. Whole books have been written trying to reconcile the belief in a benevolent and powerful God with the reality of evil and violence in the world. I am not going to try to give you a formula for resolving this apparent paradox. No formula could capture the question's subtlety and complexity, and none would satisfy you. I am simply going to tell you that you are by no means alone. Neither are you wrong for having those questions and feelings.

Anger at God is a significant spiritual and theological crisis. Again, I urge you to find one or more spiritual teachers or guides—a clergy member, a lay spiritual director, a spiritual advisor, maybe a therapist, a guru, whomever you are called to consult—and share your struggle.

Maybe your best help will come from the writings of others. As with all other kinds of help you may seek, listen to your intuition. If you do not feel you can trust what is offered to you, or you are not being trusted, if the answers you are given do not ring true or seem too simplistic, or if you feel pressure or alienation in any way, move on until you find the right resource to help you. As you become more and more clear about the precise nature of your spiritual struggle, you will find the right person or persons to guide you though it.

Many or all of your beliefs are likely to change. Maybe you will discover a new and more meaningful connection to God. Maybe you will become atheist or at least agnostic. Maybe you will move through several different perspectives. Just do not be surprised if every aspect of your spirituality is challenged as you heal from violence. Take the challenge seriously and give yourself time to work through it.

Do not be surprised if every aspect of your spirituality is challenged as you heal from violence.

Let me pass on to you a story told by a Catholic priest that may give you a perspective on these questions. This priest describes a time when he was pastor to a farming community heavily damaged by a tornado. The farmers were devastated and angry. One farmer demanded to know, "Where is God in all this?" thinking God had entirely abandoned the community. Another farmer answered, "Well, the Smiths brought us dinner, and the Joneses brought us tarps, and the folks in the next town brought back our sheep that had run away."

The first farmer thought for a long time. By remembering these acts of service, he was able to answer his own question. He could see where his God actually had been there, even in the storm's darkness. Look for what or who in your world touches your spirit; what you see may well be a manifestation of the presence of God.

Look for what touches your spirit; what you see may well be a manifestation of the presence of God.

The short version of how I dealt with anger at God

Simply put, I learned to value wholeness more than goodness.

This is a pretty radical perspective if you think about it. I came to it quite gradually. Wholeness means everything—all the dark, ugly, contemptible, difficult parts of life as well as the beautiful, awe-inspiring, light and gentle parts. I have slowly learned to accept and value the world in total, including both its light and its darkness.

I see violence as part of the sacred whole of Creation, whether I like it or not.

This is not to say I condone violence; I absolutely do not. I hate it as much as ever. But I also no longer see it as separate from my world. Rather, I see violence as part of the sacred whole of Creation, whether I like it or not. Creation includes all of what is. As that idea sank in, it changed everything for me. I believe life is an all-or-nothing deal. You cannot have just the happy half of it. Reality is an all or nothing deal, and ultimately, I believe, God is an all-or-nothing deal, too.

I am more aware now of how all parts of Creation are profoundly connected. I view my own part in combating evil as bringing as much consciousness into the world as I am able. As I face the truth of myself and the world as best I can, including the dark and unwanted parts, paradoxically I feel more authentically connected to God and my anger diminishes.

Dealing with spiritual crisis takes deeply personal inner work. Your path will not be the same as my path. I reiterate: Seek until you find a teacher or teachers who can guide you. Find your own reconciliation and understanding so you can make peace within yourself and know in your heart what is spiritually true for you.

~~~~

To summarize, many tools are available to you for your spiritual healing. Among them are meditation, prayer, religion, acceptance, developing patience, engaging in service, and expressing gratitude. Whenever times feel particularly rough, use one or more of these tools to regain your balance.

"Except for the point, the still point, there would be no dance,
and there is only the dance."
~ *T.S. Eliot,* The Four Quartets

"One does not become enlightened by imagining figures of light,
but by making the darkness conscious."
~ *C.G. Jung, CW 13:335*

"If the only prayer you said in your whole life was, 'thank you,'
that would suffice.
~ *Meister Eckhart*

Exercises for Chapter 6

These exercises are designed to help you understand and deepen your spirituality.

Actions you can take

1. **Build a spiritual practice into your life.** Spend time every day being fully and consciously present. Stop for at least 10 minutes once a day and turn your attention inward. A simple way is to meditate by sitting in silence and allowing your thoughts to flow over you, neither retaining nor resisting them. You can focus on your breath or on the sounds around you. Pray, if that is your path. Do not beat yourself up if you miss a day or your mind wanders. Simply return gently to the practice you intended.

2. **Stay alert for opportunities to serve others.** Offer your help whenever you see someone struggling. At the very least, offer a smile and maybe an encouraging word to someone you do not know. Look for ongoing volunteer opportunities in your community and commit to one or more.

3. **Create a gratitude journal.** Make entries every day. I suggest a minimum of three entries each day. Write down three things or

three people you are grateful for and why. Even when you have to stretch to find something or someone, make the entries.

Questions to ponder

1. **What is sacred to you?** What nourishes your spirit? When do you feel awe and wonder? What gives you a sense of reverence and connection to something greater than yourself?

2. **When have you learned to accept something that was difficult for you to accept?** How did acceptance feel to you? What is difficult for you to accept now? How would your life be different if you could accept all things?

7

Let Go and Make Peace

You may think that being done, making peace, and letting go are truly wrong-headed because there is no way you are ever going to be able to let the memory of violence go. In some ways you are right. Assault, violence, and rape change your life in ways that do not go away. You will not forget what happened. But you can still let go.

True, you have changed and cannot go back. There will be a time, however, when you will be done with much of your healing and will be ready, at last, to release what happened to you. Think of it more as loosening the grip of violence, letting it let go of you. Releasing is a choice you make when the time is right, when the crisis has passed.

Like everything else in healing, letting go will be different for each person. My hope is this general outline will help you envision how letting go eventually is possible.

You have changed

Let me tell you some ways you have been changed, if only to let you know these happen to nearly everyone. You are neither alone nor wrong when you recognize these changes in you.

Your physical nervous system has changed, and you now react to life situations differently. Maybe you jump at certain sounds. Perhaps darkness now scares you. Maybe you have experienced post-traumatic stress disorder and have even been treated for it, but there are some residual reactions in you to anything that reminds you of your attack. A growing number of therapists and doctors agree there is a real physical consequence of assault and trauma beyond the immediate injuries, and some physical change may be permanent. If you were raped, you may not want a sexual relationship again for a long time, even if you are married. If you were beaten, you may not want to be touched.

Your image of yourself has changed. You will never again be a person to whom violence has not happened. For a while, and maybe a fairly long while, part of your identity was "victim." The police may have referred to you that way. As I said earlier, I have personally come to hate that word and will not use it unless I have to in order to be clear. As your healing has progressed, you have felt stronger and healthier, but you now know the place inside of you where your vulnerability resides.

You now know the place inside of you where your vulnerability resides.

Your sense of safety has changed. Maybe you do not want to do certain things—to walk on a particular street, go out alone, or wear certain kinds of clothes. As I wrote earlier, I could not live on the ground floor of any building for more than 10 years. I needed to have a hallway and another locked door between my home's front door and the outside world. In the course of healing, you have discovered what you need in order to feel safe, and now you plan your life to ensure you have what you need.

Your ability to trust has probably changed. You are no longer as naive as perhaps you once were. You know about dangers others may not see. You are cautious in ways you were not before—in your actions and in your relationships. You very likely trust yourself more and the world less than you did before.

You know about dangers others may not see.

Your beliefs about your future have changed. Maybe you were faced with a long physical recovery from the attack. Your physical abilities may be different now. You may want different things from life, as your values very likely have changed. You place a higher value on the things that fed your spirit, and make you feel well and whole again, and less value on the things that feed your ego and make you feel self-important or admired.

Letting go simply means creating your new normal. This new normal will include both your memories and all you have gained in your healing process. Letting go does not mean the end of healing. Healing will go on deep within you for the rest of your life. Letting go means turning your attention in new directions.

Knowing when you are ready to let go and make peace

I believe you will be able to know with certainty when the time to let go arrives. Some part of you will know you do not want or need to keep the memory of violence in the forefront of your life anymore. No matter how terrible your experience was, the day comes when you are ready for it to take its place as just another one of your memories. You are sick of it. Deep down you know you are so much more than what happened to you. You feel ready and eager to have greater peace inside you. You have other work to do in the world—other parts of life you want to experience. Importantly, you refuse to let the perpetrator of violence against you have any more of your focus and your life's energy. Having processed and assimilated everything you need from the experience, you are ready to move on.

The time for letting go will not come all at once. Readiness to let go sort of sneaks up on you. Likewise, the letting go itself will not take place all at once, either. What happens in letting go and making peace is you shift into a new process—your process of release. Like healing and recovery, letting go takes time, too.

Like healing and recovery, letting go takes time.

You will probably not be ready to let go for quite a while. I believe the minimum time of healing after a violent attack is one to two years. More likely, the necessary time will be something like five to 10 years, and maybe 20 or more. The right time to move on is when you know you are ready, no matter how many years have passed. If you never feel ready but you continue to heal, that is okay, too.

What readiness feels like

So what does it feel like to be ready to let go and make peace? For me, it was the awareness one day that I was thoroughly sick and tired of having thoughts of rape intrude on my days. I was becoming exhausted by the whole idea. I had countered my denial with awareness and knew I was no longer denying any part of my experience. I had engaged in therapy, and it felt complete. I did not want any of my relationships with men to have even a hint of the rescuer and damsel-in-distress dynamic.

Once in a while I would realize I had not thought about my rape at all for a while. Letting go was already happening.

There was no longer a "charge" on my memory of rape. Earlier, eight years after I was raped, I found my hand shaking when I told someone new about what had happened. Even when I no longer felt consciously nervous talking about it anymore, my hands still shook every time. Then my hands stopped shaking, but when I talked, I would still feel queasy inside, feeling a flutter in my stomach and a tightening of my jaw. I knew I was ready to move on when my body stopped having all those reactions. I had processed the memory thoroughly the way my body processes food. I had integrated it and incorporated it into my overall psychological and spiritual being. I was changed, and I was done with the period of crisis.

I can promise you there will be a day for you when you can truly let go and make peace with your memories. You will not miss it. You will know that day when it comes.

But I need to feel better now!

I realize asking you to be patient may feel discouraging. As I wrote about earlier, if you are like me, you want to get back to "normal" fast, feel like you felt before the attack happened, make it all just go away. After a few days or weeks have passed, you may even be tempted to try to ignore your experience, take up your old routines, and act *as if* nothing happened.

That "as if" is the problem. Something *did* happen, and you cannot "un-happen" it. If you pretend you are beyond your experience, as I did for quite a long while and as my diabetic client in Chapter 5 did, you are likely to feel increasingly alienated from the people around you and ultimately from yourself. You will feel as if you are in a transparent bubble. You can hear and see what is going on, but you are only observing your life rather than participating in it. That hurts!

Most survivors need to experience at least one complete annual cycle to fully see the impact violence has had on them. You need to see your birthday, your anniversary, each season, and every significant holiday. Each time you will feel something you have not felt before.

Most survivors need to experience at least one complete annual cycle to fully see the impact violence has had.

You may remember past birthdays when you were happy and active, and feel now a black cloud has stopped over your head and darkened even the day that used to be your favorite. Your spirits may sink as the season gets colder and the days get shorter, or you may feel more alienated from the world of "normal" when the days get longer and the season turns to warmth. You may not feel the same kind of joy in holidays that used to give you great pleasure.

With the losses I experienced and from what I have seen in my clients, more than one annual cycle has to happen before the effects of violence begin to diminish significantly. Those effects absolutely will diminish, but it does take time—again, probably more time than you wish. Turn to your journal or mantras to keep you going. I eventually took comfort in knowing, and deeply believing, I would feel peace someday. That comfort grew in strength and outshone any frustration or impatience I felt.

In simple terms: Healing takes what it takes. You have no real choice but to be patient. Anything else will only prolong your pain. Stay the course, trust your process, and you will heal. You will come to the time when you can let go.

How to let go

Like everything else in healing, how you let go will also be different for each person. The techniques and exercises described earlier in this book can still be used in the process of letting go. Following are three more ways of letting go—tools, if you will. I have employed these tools myself. Some of my clients have found them to be transformative when the time was right for them. They are surrender, forgiveness, and ritual.

Surrender

When you have been victimized by violence, the idea of "surrender" may sound as repugnant as it can possibly sound. When you were assaulted, you may have been forced to submit to all kinds of powerlessness. You may have been forced to do things, or say things, or feel things that every particle of your being rejected. You want control back. How on earth, you may want to ask, can surrender—which can feel like the opposite of control—be part of a path toward healing?

Surrender does not mean submission, nor does it mean passivity, weakness, or giving up. Surrender is a profound form of acceptance, a letting go of your conscious ego's demands. To surrender is simply to stop fighting reality, to stop demanding or expecting something other than what is. The apparent paradox is no matter how terrible reality is or seems to be, surrendering to it in this way, through deep acceptance, diminishes the terror inside you. A higher part of you, what Carl Jung called the Self, steps in to guide you when your ego steps aside.

<hr>

Surrender is a profound form of acceptance.

<hr>

None of these ideas about surrender mean you do not work for justice, for fairness, or for any of your other values. There is nothing in the notion of surrender that means ignoring what can be improved, resolved, or made more peaceful in the world or in your life. I strongly believe in taking action toward social justice. When I do so at this point in my life, however, I stay alert for any signs my ego is becoming "hooked" into demanding, expecting, or judging. I now know these hooks or attachments are damaging *to me,* and I remind myself how much more powerful surrender is. I literally open my hands, palms up, as a physical reminder that I must let go of my demands and expectations if I am to succeed at making anything better. Acceptance and surrender are an ongoing practice for me now.

What does surrender look like, then?

My experience described in the last chapter—the moment I fell to the floor and declared somebody or something simply had to help me if I was to go on living even one more minute—was surrender. In that moment I knew I had utterly exhausted all my conscious, ego-based resources: my plans, my techniques, my tricks, my ways of losing myself, soothing myself, or forgetting. None were enough to keep me going. That was the hard truth of my situation. My ego surrendered. It was, in a way, a last step in my healing from the violence nearly 30 years earlier. I placed my full trust in something beyond myself.

A somewhat more trivial, popular illustration of surrender takes place in the second *Star Wars* movie, of all places. I think George Lucas must have a firm grasp of several spiritual principles. Luke Skywalker, having been trained by the master Yoda on the ways of the Force, was called into a fierce battle with the Empire's warriors. The odds against him and the complexity of the challenge facing him were beyond what he could possibly do physically. He simply could not maneuver his craft precisely enough to survive where he would have to fly, and he could not react quickly enough to avoid being hit and destroyed by the assailants' weapons. His ordinary way of being was at its limit, and the situation called for more.

Then the voice within him reminded him to "use the Force." He closed his eyes in the midst of battle as a sign of his willingly letting go of control and placing his trust in the Force. He surrendered. He survived and completed his mission. The Force is just another name, albeit a science fictional one, for that which responds when you surrender.

The 12-step programs for recovering from alcoholism and other addictions are another illustration. The first three steps lead to surrender. At the first step, one admits one is powerless over whatever the addictive substance or compulsive activity is. Then in the second step, one comes to believe there is a power greater than oneself that can restore sanity (can bring healing). The third step is to make a decision to turn one's will and one's life over to the care of that power (a decision to surrender). These programs have been successful for millions in breaking the grip of addiction and dealing with the underlying pain.

I note especially that second step: "We came to believe…." In that phrase is the key recognition that time is needed—that healing and believing are processes. The decision and ability to surrender come only after other concrete healing work has already been done (in this case, sobriety or abstinence). All of these programs are careful to allow their members to relate to their "power greater than ourselves" as each member understands that power to be. It need not be God or any similar understanding. No dogma, no orthodoxy, no belief is required. Even atheists are healed in AA. Surrender and concrete action are the healers.

> ## The decision and ability to surrender come only after other concrete healing work has already been done.

At the end of each sitting at the meditation center I frequently attend, we close by bowing while the person leading reads this: "To bow is to no longer hold ourselves apart from the unpredictable nature of our lives. It is to cultivate a heart that can unconditionally welcome all things. We bow to what is, to all of life," from Christina Feldman in *Buddha's Daughters: Women Who Are Shaping Buddhism in the West.* Feldman follows later in the same paragraph: "The bow is a way to the end of suffering." This quote captures the essence of surrender for me. I offer the suggestion of this way to you.

Forgiveness

If surrender seems hard, forgiveness probably seems even harder. There is one big thing to know about forgiveness: Forgiveness is something you do *for yourself,* for your own well-being, and not for the good of anyone else. It is not the same as condoning. It is not the same as tolerating, and it is not the same as forgetting. When you forgive, you do not start pretending nothing happened or what happened was okay. There is nothing in forgiveness that calls on you to deny any truth of your life.

> ## Forgiveness is something you do *for yourself.*

In 2006, the world saw a profound illustration of forgiveness in action when a gunman entered an Amish school in Pennsylvania and shot 10 girls, killing five, and then fatally shot himself. In the aftermath of grieving, many of the Amish, including parents of the dead girls, reached out in forgiveness to the shooter's mother in her grief. They even attended the shooter's funeral. The shooter's mother acknowledged that their gesture's healing power left her speechless. She said, "There are no words to describe how that made us feel that day."

In later interviews, one Amish woman was asked by a reporter how she and her community were able to get over what happened so quickly. She responded that they were not at all "over" it. She said forgiveness and the acts that embodied forgiveness simply made it possible for there to be a future for her beyond the horror. Forgiveness means no longer carrying the burden of negativity—hate, rage, contempt, fear. Forgiveness creates space inside you for positive growth. It frees your energy to attend to your own continued healing. It makes a future possible.

Forgiveness creates space inside you for positive growth.

I do not pretend forgiveness is easy; it is not. In fact, I think forgiveness is perhaps the ultimate spiritual task, taking all the health, maturity, and grace one can muster. Even then, forgiving can be difficult. It cannot be forced. You cannot just will forgiveness to happen. The actions of forgiveness, however, like those of the Amish in Pennsylvania, can be undertaken while the healing process is still continuing.

Mahatma Gandhi wrote, "The weak can never forgive. Forgiveness is the attribute of the strong." Martin Luther King, Jr. said, "We must develop and maintain the capacity to forgive. He who is devoid of the power to forgive is devoid of the power to love." It may be that all you can do now, or even long after you were attacked, is *intend* to forgive someday. I believe if your intention is sincere, it is enough and you will, in fact, find yourself forgiving someday. In forgiving, you free yourself.

Ritual

I have long appreciated rituals. I find them to be healing and sometimes transformative. A personal ritual that speaks to what you want to acknowledge or change in your life can actually help move your life in your desired direction. You may want to create for yourself a ritual around letting go.

When I use the term "ritual" I do not mean simply habit or routine. Brushing your teeth is a morning ritual for most people, but that is not what I'm talking about. I define ritual as an intentional action symbolizing in the outer physical world an inner, psycho-spiritual state or change. Ritual makes the fact of change real to your body. It is something you do mindfully to mark the changes you have made inside.

Ritual is something you do mindfully to mark the changes you have made inside.

Ritual also allows others to witness the fact that your change has taken place and honors the change. A ritual of letting go is something you do to mark your passage out of the initial stages of healing and into the long-term, more peaceful steady state of your life after violence.

Religions use ritual all the time to evoke feelings of reverence or awe, to celebrate a change in someone's status, such as a marriage, and to create and reinforce community. In a ritual, the symbols used are chosen to resonate in the emotions and spirits of those who are present. Ringing a bell, sounding a chime or gong, lighting candles, exchanging rings, sharing a service of communion or a meal, music—these are all part of familiar rituals. So are placing flowers on a grave and spinning a prayer wheel and making a pilgrimage to a sacred site.

If you choose to create a ritual of letting go for yourself, think about what resonates symbolically for you. What images come to your mind when you think about letting go? Some have used fire to burn a symbol of what is being released. Fire is an ancient representation of spirit. Burning can symbolize turning something into spirit as smoke. Many years after I was raped, I burned my master to-do list from the immediate aftermath. It was my way of releasing those early days of intense fear and anger.

Some have used water for rituals of release. I like to use the trick paper magicians use. On the paper, I write whatever I wish to release, such as the name of my fear, my dependency, my anger, or whatever part of me I am ready to let go of. Then I place the paper in a bowl of water and swirl the water. The paper dissolves quickly and completely, the ink disperses and disappears, and the words are simply gone. The water remains clear, a very satisfying image of release to my mind.

Some have used the earth by burying something symbolic of what is being released. I once helped someone bury ashes after she had concluded a difficult divorce by burning her former marriage certificate. She said she felt lighter and more free when she had finished the burying.

Some use air by filling a balloon with helium and writing on it with a felt tip pen. Letting go of the balloon's string is yet another gesture of release. You can watch the balloon drift slowly up and away from you until it is no longer visible. With it, the words written on it disappear as well, analogous to the slow process of healing.

Ritual's function of creating community is served by inviting witnesses to your ritual. Be careful to include only those who know you well, who will understand why you have chosen to create a ritual, and who can be there to support you and participate in the way you want them to. This is your community in your healing process. Do your ritual in solitude if that feels more correct to you. Ritual is yet another time when you need to trust your instincts and intuition.

~ ~ ~ ~

There will be a day when you are ready to release the urgent intensity of your experience with violence. You cannot hurry that day, but you also will not miss it. Even though the violent acts committed against you may have been terrible and extremely damaging, when the time is finally right, the spiritual tools of surrender, forgiveness, and ritual can give you a needed and profound sense of peaceful completion.

"This is one of the hidden gifts of serious illness or loss.
It pushes us right to our edge, where we may have the good fortune to realize
that our only real option is to surrender to our experience and let it just be."
~ Ezra Bayda

Exercises for Chapter 7

These exercises are designed to remind you letting go comes at the end of a major shift in your consciousness.

Actions you can take

1. **Re-read this chapter periodically.** Think of this chapter as a map you can look at to see where you are going. Pay particular attention to the section on thinking you need to feel better right away to remind yourself healing requires patience and acceptance.

2. **Meditate on forgiveness or surrender.** Let these ideas turn in your mind and heart. Let their meaning seep into you. Do not try to hurry either idea. Notice how your meditation changes over time.

3. **Decide whether you want to create any ritual(s) and what it or they would be.** What comes up for you when you think about a ritual? Are there particular images you find especially meaningful? What will it mean to you to mark a point in time as a transition to your peacefully letting go?

Questions to ponder

1. **How do you feel when you are "hooked" and attached to something?** How is your body different when you are demanding, expecting, or judging something? What signs do you see in yourself when you are attached?

2. **When do you feel most peaceful inside?** What gives you peace? What thoughts tend to disrupt your sense of peace? What helps you recover inner peace?

8

A Note for Friends, Partners,

and Families

A particularly bad time for me came when my closest friend became exhausted and expressed it as anger—actually rage—toward me. She suddenly lashed out verbally one evening about two months after my rape, telling me I was making too many demands on her (all things she had offered), was a terrible burden (setting off shame in me), and was "too sick for [her] to handle." I felt a profound sense of abandonment and a whole new round of fear and embarrassment. I started thinking of myself as "sick" when, as I now know, I was only experiencing the normal level of emotional pain that follows violence. Ultimately, she was as devastated as I was by the darkness that had passed between us. We both found it difficult to repair the relationship. The friendship, in fact, never entirely recovered, and eventually we lost touch with each other.

If you are the friend, partner, or a family member of someone who has experienced violence, yours is a challenging role. The person who was attacked is, in some ways, lost to you for a while. She or he must devote all her attention and energy to coping with her changed situation and beginning her process of healing. She or he cannot "be there" for you, but you *can* "be there" for her.

The person who was attacked is, in some ways, lost to you for a while.

As time passes, she or he will gradually return. As the survivor slowly becomes herself again—or her new self—your relationship will come back to something like what it was. You will again have a more reciprocal connection, will probably be more joyful, and will find your relationship more fulfilling for both of you. You will come back to living more in present time. So how do you help someone heal after violence and come back to you? What pitfalls do you want to avoid?

What the survivor needs most from you

From my own experience and from the stories I have heard from clients, there are three things most survivors of violence need:

1. They need **to be heard and believed.** They need their story to be listened to, understood, and accepted.

2. They need **control.** They need to feel back in charge of their own lives.

3. They need **practical, concrete help.**

They do not need to be cheered up. They do not need to put their experience "in perspective." That will come much later, if ever. They do not need advice unless you know about something factual they actually do not know. They may or may not need to spend time alone, but they definitely do not need to feel abandoned, avoided, or stigmatized. People with the courage to walk beside them are of great value—people who neither lead nor are afraid, and certainly who do not judge or blame them. Survivors need to feel fully human, fully accepted, and fully supported. Throughout the time of healing, every survivor needs hope.

Survivors need to feel fully human, fully accepted, and fully supported.

Listening

Coaches and therapists talk about three levels of listening. Most of us are familiar with the first level, but the other two are more important when you are supporting a survivor.

The first level of listening is what happens in an ordinary exchange of information. I say what I want to say, then you say what you want to say, then back to me. While you are talking, I am probably half processing what you are saying and half planning what I am going to say when my turn comes. I may even get so excited about my own ideas or story that I interrupt your turn and start talking right away. My goal, and probably yours as well, is to hear what I have to say and get you to hear me, too. If you are listening to me this way, I can see it in your eyes and feel it my heart. This familiar way of listening is not what a survivor needs from you, I'm sorry to say.

The second level of listening is when I forget about myself and become immersed in what you have to say. I let myself visualize what you are telling me and imagine what feelings you must have had. One key to second level listening is curiosity. Many of us avoid this type of listening because we are afraid we will seem "nosy," but there is a big difference between curious and nosy. Being nosy is when I want information for my own purposes—to judge or evaluate, to categorize, to feel superior, to dismiss or minimize, to manipulate you to do something. Being curious is when I just want to understand; I do not want to judge or evaluate or use your experience in any way.

When I am listening at the second level, my goals are to comprehend what you are telling me and to experience your world vicariously. In order to understand, I need to be open to recognizing what I do not know, to caring, and to wondering.

A survivor may need to tell her or his story many times over many weeks. One of the best things you can offer is a willing ear to listen fresh each time.

Part of the second level of listening is patience. I have to let you tell your story in your own way, at your own pace, and I have to let you repeat yourself as many times as you feel the need to repeat. A survivor may need to tell her or his story many times over many weeks. One of the best things you can offer is a willing ear to listen fresh each time.

The facts about an experience of violence may be simple and quickly told. The full truth of the experience, however, cannot as easily be conveyed. The depth of fear or pain, the extent of grief and sadness, the anger, the confusion, any guilt or shame—all these are processed over time through many re-tellings. Science now recognizes part of a survivor's brain (the *amygdala*) stores the memory of trauma and requires the survivor to go over the experience many times in order to integrate it and make peace with it. Only someone listening at this second level can hear what a survivor needs to tell.

The third level of listening is when I notice what is *not* being said and sense the atmosphere—the "energy," if you will—behind the words I hear. If you relate the sequence of events you experienced but never mention any emotion, directly or indirectly, I hear several things at the third listening level.

I hear you are either not in touch yet with what you feel, you cannot put it into words, you do not trust me enough to say it to me, or you refuse to let yourself feel anything right now. I can tell at this level whether you are tense and hiding something (your speech may be halting, your eyes are darting around, you are biting your lip or placing your hand over your mouth) or whether you are unaware of what you are not saying, exhibiting no tension but rather signaling you think you are telling all. I may not know exactly what is hidden, but I know something definitely *is* going on and is not being said.

One important thing to remember as a friend, partner, or family member is this. Your job is not to make your friend or partner aware of what she or he is avoiding saying. You might be wrong. Even if you're "right," you cannot know the survivor's timing or pace of healing. Each survivor needs to uncover her or his own truth in her or his own way and never needs you to impose your interpretation, ideas, or assessment, no matter how well intended you may be.

Granting control

The essence of violence is taking control away from the victim or survivor. That, in fact, is the exact point of violence. The perpetrator has all the control, and something about having control is what motivates him or her in the first place. Consider these scenarios. He blocked her from leaving. He tied her up. He gagged her so she could not be heard. He forced her body to do things she did not want to do. He punched, cut, or stabbed her, and she could not stop him or protect herself. Not only did the survivor lose control, but in many cases, the perpetrator deliberately intensified the experience of helplessness and lack of control by repeatedly drawing attention to it.

As a result, one thing every survivor needs is to be back in control. As a support person, your role is to help your friend or partner, not to direct. The survivor really does know best what she or he can tolerate at any given time. Even if you think you know what she or he needs to do (e.g., go to the police, go to the hospital, move away, get rid of a relationship—whatever it is you think) if you want to be of real help, you will be quiet. At most, state your opinion and then relinquish control back to the survivor. You have to believe deep down that whatever she or he decides to do is all right. The great gift you can give to a survivor is to stay without judgment, no matter what she or he decides to do. Again, remember that getting back control is paramount for their healing.

The great gift you can give to a survivor is to stay without judgment, no matter what she or he decides to do.

Keeping your opinions to yourself can be very tough. I drove my friends nearly crazy when I refused to go to the police for three days after I was raped. I know they struggled to do nothing more than suggest I go. Had any of them pushed me into a car and taken me to the police station, however, they would have done harm to the fragile structure of healing I was just beginning to build inside me. They likely would have lost my friendship forever. Yes, I have pretty high needs for autonomy and control in my life, so my reactions might have been somewhat extreme, but I have heard clients report the same thing. They tell me they could not tolerate the idea of someone making them do *anything* in the aftermath of violence.

Your curiosity is not the survivor's obligation.

Part of granting control is granting a survivor the right *not* to tell the story. Your curiosity is not the survivor's obligation. Men in particular frequently find it difficult to talk about having been assaulted, for a whole range of cultural and psychological reasons. The vulnerability and loss of control inherent in violence can be extremely shameful for a man. He may fear his masculinity is in question because he was victimized. His fears are not unfounded. Others may, in fact, think differently about him. As we saw in Chapter 5, one group serving male survivors reported the average amount of time before a male victim tells his story is 20 years. Twenty is just an average; many men keep their experience to themselves for many more years.

Women, too, can find it quite challenging to talk about what happened to them. Everything from shame to fear to guilt can work to keep a woman silent. Her need to be connected to others is still there, but the forces operating against talking can be more powerful for a while, maybe for a long time. You, as a friend or partner, can signal your willingness to listen and then must wait until the survivor feels the time is right and you are the right one to hear. A simple "I know this was awful for you, and I am here to listen whenever, if ever, you want to talk" is enough. Then wait.

The kind of help you can give

You will need to strike a balance between helping the person you care about and allowing her or him privacy. Because each situation and each person are unique, you will need to rely on your intuition, observation, and the direct messages you get from your friend or partner to find that balance.

Still, in the aftermath of violence, a great many practical details must be attended to. It can be a significant help if the burden is shared. For example, you can drive your friend or family member to appointments with doctors, police, or lawyers. You can simply handle some of the paperwork; fill out forms and reports and maybe insurance claims. If the survivor needs to get new clothes, you can take her or him shopping. You can prepare nutritious meals or include her or him in your meals. You can research the names and contact information for possible support groups, spiritual counselors, addiction support groups, or other resources. Just be sensitive to what your offerings may imply.

Most importantly, you can give her or him the right to say *no* to whatever you offer without you becoming angry or hurt. I had one client tell me how her friends seemed to want to help by managing everything for her, including scheduling appointments without consulting her, preparing food and demanding she eat it, and, worst of all, telling her she "should" focus on the future and put her assault behind her. She felt discounted, abandoned, and more alone than if she actually had been alone.

Here are some simple do's and don'ts when you want to be supportive to a survivor.

What not to do

From my own experience and from the stories of my clients, I have seen or heard of most mistakes helpers inadvertently make. These are the main ones. I mention them here to help you be aware and avoid them.

- **Do not make demands.** This follows from what I said above about granting control and respecting the survivor's timing and process. Do not insist the survivor go anywhere, do anything, or share anything. If possible, do not even mention or show in your face that you have any expectation of what "should" happen. Genuine acceptance and openness are healing; expectations are not.

> Genuine acceptance and openness are healing; expectations are not.

The one exception is if you suspect your friend or family member is contemplating suicide or other physical self-harm. Sometimes survivors of violence do have such thoughts. In this case, I believe you, as a support person, are justified in being pushy and doing everything you can to connect your friend with professional help.

There is still a balance to be struck. If you force something to happen, you risk diminishing your friend's much-needed sense of control. If, however, you do nothing, you risk your friend acting on suicidal impulses. Use your best judgment at the moment. Keep your heart open and act out of your caring, not your intellectual or moral sense of what is "right." Your caring intention will make a difference and help you find the balance. Your friend is also more likely to accept your actions if she or he can sense authentic caring in you.

- **Do not be blinded by your expectations.** Because we all live in a culture distorted in the way it deals with violence and its victims, you may hold some stereotypes that you are not even aware of. Let me tell you another story.

During my own healing, I volunteered with a rape prevention and treatment center at the YWCA. As part of that work, I taught one session of an advanced officer training course at the local police department. This was a fairly enlightened police department in a highly educated college town. Still, the images the officers carried in their minds of a rape victim tended to come more from television and movies—images of sobbing, trembling, shattered women.

I was told one of my greatest contributions was to wake them up to the reality that bright, educated women do not generally act in the stereotypical way. The cooler behavior of these women, however, does not mean they are not in pain. It also does not mean the crime did not happen. Instead, such women tend to intellectualize their experience. They may appear cold and unmoved, even when they feel shattered inside. Without awareness of how expectations operate, some officers might not have taken the crimes against the women in their town as seriously.

Ask yourself what you expect survivors of violence to act like. Really think about where you got those expectations. Do they come from the media? Have you had experience with someone else that has shaped your expectations now? Do you believe a survivor "should" cry or shake or explode in anger?

Ask yourself whether your loved one is *ever* likely to act in the way you expect. How has she or he reacted to lesser difficulties in the past? If your loved one is a very quiet, private person, she or he is not likely to demonstrate strong emotions visibly, no matter what happened. If she or he is a more extroverted person in general, you may see more overt and dramatic signs. What you see on the outside does not tell you much about what is happening inside a survivor. Being mindful of your own expectations will help you respond to your friend or partner more authentically and compassionately.

What you see on the outside does not tell you much about what is happening inside a survivor.

• **Do not ask your friend or partner to be happy, peaceful, hopeful, or optimistic any time soon.** Healing after violence takes most of a survivor's energy for a very long time. Many of our positive emotions are aimed at the future and expectations of better times to come. Your friend or partner may find those positive emotional states impossible for some time. Survivors often experience a time of disconnection and a combination of fear and grief. Furthermore, a survivor's moods are usually not stable. They may swing from one emotion to another rapidly. All those reactions are entirely normal and predictable—and they do not last forever. You may still share laughter or even momentary playfulness. Hope for the future may come and go. Your friend will not necessarily fall into clinical depression. You, as the supporter, must be open and accepting of whatever happens.

Your friend or partner may find those positive emotional states impossible for some time.

• **Do not "rescue." Do not "parent."** A survivor does not need another mother or father, nor a hero or heroine to tell her or him what to do or handle the world for her or him. Remember: Survivors need to regain control, and they need respect. If you emotionally put yourself in a superior position of any sort—the knight in shining armor rushing in to save the fair maiden or the all-knowing, all-capable parent who takes over and makes it all better—you diminish the survivor and deprive her or him of the renewed control she or he needs.

What to do instead

There are three overall bits of guidance I hope to give to you who are supporters. These are the things I wished those around me had known and many of my clients have expressed in their wishes.

• **Do your own healing work.** I cannot emphasize this one too much. If someone close to you has been victimized by violence, you can be certain something has happened inside you as well. It may have triggered some of your own fears. If you cannot face those, you could end up abandoning your friend. It may have triggered your anger, but your loved one may not be able to be around any form of anger in the aftermath of violence. My father, for example, wanted to hunt down and kill the man who raped me, but I could not even listen to him talk that way. I understood it intellectually, but the mere thought of more violence was unbearable to me.

Your loved one's experience may have triggered some kind of guilt or shame in you. Maybe you are concerned you were not able to prevent or stop the assault against someone you love. You may feel at a loss for words or distressed you are not able to solve anything. You need to heal these rips in the fabric of your own being before you can be fully supportive to your loved one.

For your own healing, you can also use the strategies described in the rest of this book. Become aware of what you are saying to yourself and what stories you are telling yourself. Stay aware of your own physical and emotional needs, from your needs for food and sleep to your own need for a compassionate listener. Take care to get your needs met as you are helping your loved one.

Take care to get your needs met as you are helping your loved one.

If you sacrifice any of your own needs, you are likely to feel resentful eventually. Attend to your own spiritual needs through worship, meditation, prayer, service, and gratitude—whatever fits for you. Make sure you spend private time for yourself. Either alone or with others, do something you find light and fun, such as watching a movie or listening to music, so you do not become exhausted with your survivor friend's situation.

- **Find your own outlets.** Do not underestimate the importance of getting your own needs met. You still need friends, but your friend who survived violence cannot be your sounding board or support right now. Spend time with other friends who care about you. All supporters need support themselves. Maybe join a support group yourself for the partners of survivors. Consider seeing a counselor or consult with a clergy member, whomever you trust to tell about your struggle.

All supporters need support themselves.

You *must* replenish your own reserves and restore your own sense of balance when you are giving a great deal of your time and emotional energy to someone whose needs are as complex as those of a survivor. If you do not take care of yourself and your own needs, not only will you suffer but you could also do significant harm. You will not be able to stop yourself. I want you to have the insight and wisdom to be a strong help to yourself and to your partner or friend. Since you are reading this chapter, I know you want that, too. Therefore, please find your own sources of support.

• **Keep silence together.** You do not always have to be doing or saying something to be very valuable to a survivor. Sometimes simple companionship is all that is needed. Rachel Naomi Remen, a physician who teaches other physicians about healing and caring, says it beautifully:

When you offer compassionate silence, you may be offering what your loved one needs the very most.

"Perhaps the most important thing we bring to another person is the silence in us, not the sort of silence that is filled with unspoken criticism or hard withdrawal. The sort of silence that is a place of refuge, of rest, of acceptance of someone as they are. We are all hungry for this other silence. It is hard to find. In its presence we can remember something beyond the moment, a strength on which to build a life. Silence is a place of great power and healing." When you offer compassionate silence, you may be offering what your loved one needs the very most.

~ ~ ~ ~

In summary, you need not be perfect. Your clear and heartfelt intentions are enough. Your loved one will feel them. Focus on keeping your demands and expectations in check, practicing listening and acceptance as best you can, keeping silence sometimes, and tending to your own needs. With these, you can walk beside and support your loved one through the dark times as you both heal.

"I don't know the perfect thing to say when a person is hurting
but I do know the last thing they want to hear
are reasons they shouldn't be hurting."
~ Paula Heller Garland

9

To Be You Again

You have now read my insights into healing after violence. Remember: Healing is a process, not a destination. There is no real end point. As such, healing will go on for the rest of your life, and that is a good thing. You can only discover your unique way of healing as you do it. You cannot anticipate how long each phase of healing will take, and you cannot really know where all it will take you. The path of healing is a path of continual discovery. It is, however, a path you can trust, even when you do not know exactly how the path is going to unfold.

You will learn a great deal as you heal. You will learn who you are at a very deep level. You will learn what your own strength and courage feel like. Healing is an act of love. Acknowledge yourself regularly for what you are able to do to heal. Do something concrete for yourself periodically such as buying yourself flowers or a gift.

Very importantly, pay attention and notice as your life gets better. As you live more fully in present time, be aware of how you are getting stronger and how you are feeling more at peace. Look in the mirror and congratulate yourself for surviving. Tell yourself how much you really love you.

What to do when an emotional setback "emergency" comes

What if you suddenly slip into a state of mind you felt earlier: fear, anger, grief, or panic? This is not only common but I suspect inevitable. Humans do not heal in a straight line. We go forward and back, then farther forward, then a little back, and so on.

The first thing to remember is this: Do not add to your own distress by telling yourself there is something wrong with you. Do not decide you are not healing the "right" way. There is no "right" way to heal or to deal with an emotional setback. Nothing is wrong when you feel as if you have gone backward. Your healing process is simply your own process and your path will go where it will go. In the long run, your path will go forward.

There is no "right" way to heal or to deal with an emotional setback

---

What, however, if you feel really terrible again? Remember what helped you in the past and do those things again. Pull out a mantra or write a new one, and carry it with you for a while. Say it out loud several times a day. Take extra care of yourself physically by eating very nutritious food, sleeping as much as you need, and moving your body whenever you can.

Reconnect with whatever help you found earlier, whether that means returning to therapy or counseling, seeking out additional spiritual direction, going back to a support group, calling a good friend—whatever really helped you. Keep writing in your journal, expressing all the feelings running through you as honestly as you can. Tell yourself the truth in the privacy of your journal, both positive and negative. Return to your daily prayer, meditation, or other spiritual practice, or increase the number of times you meditate or pray. Write down at least one thing you are grateful for every day, without fail. Find a way to be of service to others right away. Do a small act of kindness or service to someone else every day. Remember surrender and forgiveness and how you felt when you first found them.

Be gentle and compassionate with yourself. You will move forward again because nothing stays the same, not even your negative feelings. Acceptance is especially important, over and over, when you are healing from violence.

Nothing stays the same, not even your negative feelings.

Some things do not change

I have a couple of residual reactions even now, 40 years after my rape, that tell me not everything will be restored after violence. I still consider myself healed, but I have what is like psychic scar tissue in me, a part of me that responds differently than the rest of me. Most likely, you will also find lasting reactions in yourself that are new after violence. Do not worry about them. They can be managed.

Whenever I see a knife appear suddenly in a movie or on TV or on stage, especially if it is a switchblade, I feel a sort of subtle electric shockwave go through my body for a moment, and I remember. The reaction only lasts a few seconds. I can easily move beyond it, put it aside, and return to watching the movie or play. Still, it never fails to be there. I feel that little shock every so often and am reminded that I was changed permanently on that night. I can handle it.

Palm Sunday also reminds me every year. For quite a few years, I would begin feeling anxious around early April for what I thought was no reason. I would look to my present-time circumstances to try to explain my feelings. Then after a day or two, I would usually remember what time of year it was, and it would all makes sense. My body remembers and knows that when the days lengthen, the cycle has come around again. For many years now, I have stopped being surprised by the feelings when they come each year. Those feelings are an unavoidable part of every spring for me. I make sure to take extra care of myself for those weeks and wait for the feelings to pass. Each year, they do pass.

To be you again

No matter how scattered and fractured you may have felt at first, no matter how disillusioned, afraid, enraged, or humiliated, here is the big secret: Through it all, every hour, every minute, you are never alone in the universe. You are always with yourself, and I believe you are always with a higher power.

> ## You are always with yourself, and I believe you are always with a higher power.

Slowly you will discover the wiser, stronger, more open and accepting you that you have become. New experiences and challenges will come into your life, and you will meet them with new skills and insights. You will learn what you are capable of, what you can tolerate, how you forgive, how you love, whom you can trust, and what means the most to you.

Then one day you, like me, will realize you genuinely have no need to struggle to be you again. You will know you always will be you. You will know that you always were.

~ ~ ~

"The wound is the place where the Light enters you."

~ Rumi

Appendix A

Sample Mantras

I have urged you to find one or more simple mantras you can easily remember and say to yourself to support yourself whenever you feel you need it. Here are some of mine and some that clients of mine have used. If any fit for you, use them. If you believe one of these—or you really want to believe it—use it now. If none work for you, write your own. Make it something that feels truthful to you.

Write your mantra on a piece of paper you can carry with you, or put it into your smartphone in some way so you can pull it up anytime.

1. You are more than your emotions and more than what happened to you.

2. Healing will take more time than you wish but less time than you fear.

3. Numbing out drags it out.

4. Trust your body, mind, and spirit to know how to heal.

5. Asking for help is a sign of strength.

6. Know your truth; speak your truth.

7. Forgiving is something you do for yourself, not for anyone else.

8. Helping another helps you.

9. If it is real to you, it is real.

10. Take it easy; make it easy.

11. Life is an all-or-nothing deal.

12. You can always be grateful for something.

13. You truly *can* do everything you *must* do.

Appendix B

Resources

*I*ncluded here are several resources you as a survivor of violence or those close to you may find helpful.

Crisis Lines and National Organizations

The National Domestic Violence Hotline
1-800-799-7233 (1-800-787-3224 (TTY))
www.thehotline.org
A 24-hour, seven-days-a-week crisis call line for those experiencing domestic violence. Website includes information on local resources, written publications, and videos.

National Network to End Domestic Violence
http://nnedv.org/
Website includes information on planning to leave a violent situation and on staying safe after you do.

National Sexual Assault Hotline
1-800-656-HOPE (1-800-656-4673)

A program of the Rape, Abuse & Incest National Network (RAINN). A 24-hour, seven-days-a-week crisis call line that automatically and confidentially connects callers to local rape crisis center resources. Website includes information and guidance for survivors and family and friends.

National Suicide Prevention Lifeline
1-800-273-TALK (8255) (1-800-799-4889 (TTY))

Free, confidential support for those contemplating suicide or for their family and friends. Website includes information on local resources.

Depression and Bipolar Support Alliance (DBSA)

www.dbsalliance.org.

Offers support groups for those suffering from depression or bipolar disorder and for their partners and families. Website offers contact information for local groups. Not a crisis center.

Resources for Survivors of Torture and War

The Center for Victims of Torture

(1-612-436-4855)

www.cvt.org

Provides healing services for survivors of torture and trains others to provide such support around the world. Not a crisis line.

National Center for PTSD, Veterans Administration

(1-800-273-8255—crisis line)

www.ptsd.va.gov

Serves U.S. military veterans suffering from post-traumatic stress disorder. Website offers a locator for treatment programs.

Nearly every local community has multiple sources of help available for survivors of violence. You can search online for the names and contact information of organizations where you live or visit the national websites above.

Books

These are a few of the books that have inspired me, each in a different way. They have given me insight into violence and how healing happens.

Brownmiller, Susan. *Against Our Will: Men, Women and Rape* (New York: A Fawcett Book,Ballantine Publishing Group, 1975).

Bryant-Davis, Thema. *Surviving Sexual Violence: A Guide to Recovery and Empowerment* (Lanham, MD: Rowman and Littlefield Publishers, 2014).

Francisco, Patricia Weaver. *Telling: A Memoir of Rape and Recovery* (New York: Cliff Street Books, HarperCollins Publishers, Inc., 1999).

Frankl, Viktor E. *Man's Search for Meaning* (Cuthogue, NY: Buccaneer Books, Inc., 1959; Boston, Mass.: Beacon Press, 2006).

Frederickson, Barbara L. *Positivity: Groundbreaking Research Reveals How to Embrace the Hidden Strength of Positive Emotions, Overcome Negativity, and Thrive* (New York: Crown Publishers, 2009).

Kurtz, Ernest, and Katherine Ketcham. *The Spirituality of Imperfection: Storytelling and the Search for Meaning* (New York: Bantam Books, Inc., 1992).

Meninger, William A. *The Process of Forgiveness* (New York: The Continuum Publishing Company, 1996).

Rolheiser, Ronald. *The Shattered Lantern: Rediscovering a Felt Presence of God* (New York: The Crossroad Publishing Company, 2004).

Shapiro, Francine. *Getting Past Your Past: Taking Control of Your Life with Self-Help Techniques from EMDR Therapy* (New York: Rodale, Inc., 2012).

Tolle, Eckhart. *The Power of Now: A Guide to Spiritual Enlightenment* (Novato, Calif.: New World Library, 1999).

Williams, Mary Beth, and Soili Poijula. *The PTSD Workbook: Simple, Effective Techniques for Overcoming Traumatic Stress Symptoms* (Oakland, CA: New Harbinger Publications, Inc., 2013).

Woodman, Marian, and Elinor Dickson. *Dancing in the Flames: The Dark Goddess in the Transformation of Consciousness* (New York: Shambala, 1997).

Acknowledgments

I have been blessed by many truly inspiring teachers, colleagues, and mentors. Their words and their lives have taught me about authenticity, integrity, and healing. I am especially indebted to Rosamonde Miller, Lyn Cowan, Donna Taylor, Tricia Mageli-Maley, Alain Enthoven, and the late Arthur Hastings.

I owe particular thanks to Margaret Churchill and Kathryn McGee for the insights and wisdom they shared with me after reading an earlier version of this book. Their suggestions and thoughts helped me improve the book significantly. Any remaining shortcomings are mine, not theirs.

I am grateful and humbled by all my clients who trusted me with the stories of both their pain and their triumphs.

Many true friends—some with me for a short while and some for decades—have graced my life with their courage, patience, humor, caring, and loyalty. They each brought into my life some part of the healing and wisdom I have tried to share in this book. For them I will always be thankful.

Finally, I am deeply grateful to my husband, Bob, who willingly spent hours alone while I wrote, who brought me roses when I could never have expected them, and whose support now fills my days with love.

About the Author

Patricia Drury Sidman draws from her experiences as both a professional with coaching and spiritual training and a determined rape survivor for her book To Be You Again, an uplifting guide to the healing and recovery processes for victims of violence.

Holding a BA in philosophy and an MBA with a focus on the nonprofit and public sectors from Stanford University, Sidman has worked as a health care policy analyst, business consultant, and manager.

An urge to help others in need of healing led her to become an ordained Gnostic priest in 2002 and gain certification as a professional life coach from the Coach Training Institute in 2006. Since then, she has provided life, health, and spiritual coaching to hundreds of clients, many of whom have also been survivors of violence.

Sidman lives with her husband, Bob, in Lafayette, Louisiana, where she continues to coach clients.

Made in the USA
San Bernardino, CA
02 February 2015